Spirits, Life, Worship:

A Hawaiian Religious and Catholic Perspective

D1621779

By T. Jerome Overbeck, S.J., Ph.D.

ISBN: 978-1500982676

Printed in the United States of America

Table of Contents

FOREWORD: How This Research Project Originated

I called him grandpa. When I taught his granddaughter at Santa Clara University in 1974, I had no idea that her grandfather was the high priest of the Hawaiian religion. Two years later, his granddaughter asked me to help her celebrate her Catholic wedding in Honolulu at her home parish and there I met grandpa for the first time. Though I found myself intrigued by learning that grandpa was the main *kahuna* (Keeper of the Secrets)[1] of the MO'OKINI line, I understood little about what that meant and I had no clue what surprises lay ahead.

Since I spent several weeks that same summer leading prayer at another Honolulu parish, the mother of the SCU Hawaiian bride invited me to preside at a Mass in their home for some family and friends. Grandpa was seated in the front row, next to his daughter and her husband and the grandchildren.

During the course of the liturgy, it started to rain lightly. I remember thinking: if the skies open up into a down-pour, where can we go? The *lanai* (porch) could not hold all of us and a sizable number of the assembly were older and needed places to sit. I distinctly remember saying to myself: let it go, just pray; it seems to be subsiding. After a little while, the rain dissipated.As soon as the Mass finished, grandpa did not budge. I noticed that he was staring at me intently and he motioned for me to come over to him. Since he was in his eighties and hearing clearly had become an issue, I bent down on one knee (full vestments and all) very near grandpa's face. To my surprise and bewilderment, with passion I had not seen in him before, grandpa pointed at me and with authority said: *Pono...Kahuna Pule.* I stared at grandpa a while, assuming that he had spoken Hawaiian to me, but I had no grasp of the meaning of

---

[1.] Max Freedom Long, The Science Behind Miracles. Los Angeles: Kosmon Press, 1948, p. 2.

what he said. The force of his voice and the purposefulness of his tone signaled significance beyond the ordinary. So I looked to his daughter, the mother of the SCU newlywed who was sitting next to grandpa, for help. She said: do you know what grandpa said to you? I shook my head no. She said: grandpa just gave you your Hawaiian names. Immediately I looked back at grandpa and remember thinking: I wonder if naming someone in the Hawaiian religious tradition bears significance similar to the Biblical tradition–identifying the role God gives someone within the community.[2] When I looked back at the daughter for clarification, she told me that *pono* means good.[3] Stupidly I said: just good? And she returned such an exasperated look that silenced me to really listen and attend to multiple meanings being expressed. Then she inquired whether I understood the meaning of *kahuna*. Again I offered some stupid slang, popular interpretation of the term, because that exhausted my knowledge. She told me that a kahuna was a kind of expert. When

------

[2] While many contemporary Hawaiians succumb to the current temptation of choosing a name which merely sounds melodious and rhythmical, the current high priestess of the Mo'okini line of the indigenous Hawaiian religion continues to believe (as did the Hawaiians of old) that names bear significance which affects a person's life. The name motivates and cultivates the kind of person he or she is and is becoming. The name carries the person throughout life. Personal interview with Zita Leimomi Mo'okini Lum, 5 December 2003.

Naming is extraordinarily significant in the Hawaiian tradition. A whole treatise could be written on the matter. See E.S. Craighill and Mary Kawena Pukui, The Polynesian Family System in Ka-'u, Hawaii. Wellington, N.Z.:The Polynesian Society, Inc., 1958. Also see Mary Kawena Pukui, E.W. Haertig and Catherine A. Lee, Nana I Ke Kumu (Look to the Source), Vol. One. Honolulu: Hui Hanai, Queen Lili'uokalani Children's Center, 1972.

[3] The daughter gave me a quick and easily understandable response in the situation. *Pono* can mean goodness, uprightness, righteousness, etc. See Mary Kawena Pukui and Samuel H. Elbert, Hawaiian Dictionary: Hawaiian-English, English Hawaiian (Revised and Enlarged Edition). Honolulu: University of Hawaii Press, 1986, p. 340.

she asked about my understanding of *pule*, humbly I confessed total ignorance. She explained that *pule* means pray-er, and immediately I turned to look at grandpa. Then she asked what seemed like a random question: do you know anything about Eskimos? Because I know some of our Jesuits who work in Alaska, I said that I know a little. And when she questioned me about the Eskimos' understanding of snow, I said that I knew different kinds of snow carry different kinds of significance. And she stopped me right there with a gesture. She continued that for us Hawaiians there are different kinds of rain, and the kind of rain which fell as you were praying is similar to what we Catholics would call sanctifying grace. She also said that what you may not know is that a rainbow arced you from over the mountain at that time. I got the chills when she told me this. I knew that I had not seen the rainbow, but I also knew these are not the kind of people who lie and that this time of prayer indeed was what I would call holy ground. God had visited us in a special way during that Mass.

Almost thirty years later, I continue to pray about this experience and to appropriate more of the meanings of these names. This experience and some others like it carry profound resonances in my life. Such experiences fuel the passion and respectful awe with which I approach God revealing himself in the Hawaiian context. My closest Hawaiian friends and I "talk story"[4] about these experiences and their unfolding meanings to me. To this day they call me Pono.

[4.] A common expression in the Islands which refers to telling someone stories which reveal aspects of your interior life and what they mean to you.

[A Hawaiian playing the nose flute]

"Nana 'ia i ka ho 'ole mana
Ho'ole 'ike, ho 'ole ola
Ho'ole akua e, 'a 'ohe akua
Nawai la ka 'ole o ke kua?

Let the denial of spirit power be seen
Denial of knowledge (wisdom), denial of life
Denial of deity, no deity
Who will deny deity?"[5]

[Part of an ancient Hawaiian ole (chanted prayer)]

---

5. June Gutmanis, Na Pule Kahiko: Ancient Hawaiian Prayers. Honolulu: Editions Limited, 1983, p. 112.

ACKNOWLEDGMENTS

Following this expression of gratitude and praise to God (the preceding chant, *oli*), many people provided resources which made this research project a reality. They deserve a word of acknowledgment and appreciation.

Thanks to Mr. and Mrs. Jay and Mimi Cattermole who made it possible for me to reach the Hawaiian Islands and to return safely. The inspiration of my friends, Molly Wardell, Kekoaʻikaika Satterfield, Pat Kathman and Joe Schlipman motivated me in significant ways. Thanks to Frs. John Berger and Gary Secor and the Cathedral parish in Honolulu who offered a welcoming home and community for prayer and pastoral ministry. This context helped the research and writing.

The generous staff at the Bishop Museum in Honolulu assisted in so many ways. Thanks to *Tutu* Pat (Maka) Bacon, Dr. Guy Kaulukukui, Ms. Patty Lei Belcher, Ms. Betty Kam, Ms. B.J. Short. Thanks also to Thelma G. Parish whose breadth and depth of knowledge regarding Hawaiiana amazed me again and again.

Loyola University Chicago and the Jesuits display exceptional wisdom not only to allow such a sabbatical research project, but also to offer encouragement and support. In a time and place when most companies fixate on short-term profit, the Jesuits and the University invest in me and my efforts for the longer haul– hoping I will return rested and with even more to offer for the future. Uncommonly wise leadership!

Most of all, I want to thank General Alexis and Mrs. Leimomi Lum for the countless ways their generosity and knowledge and spirit evoked a sense of awe and wonder in me. They modeled better than I have ever experienced to give freely from what we have received so freely. Thanks to their help primarily, this research project opened vistas which will serve me and hopefully many others for a lifetime. Truly they enabled this to become a work of love, whose dimensions astounded me.

INTRODUCTION: A COMPARATIVE LENS

This book examines aspects of the interior life with a comparative lens. Besides the vantage point of this contemporary Catholic, Jesuit priest-professor, the perspective of a contemporary high priestess (*kahuna nui*) of the indigenous Hawaiian religion provides a comparative lens to view spirits, life, and worship.

Zita Leimomi Mo'okini Lum is the *kahuna nui* of one of Hawaii's most sacred, oldest and largest historic sites. Located on the northern slopes of the Big Island of Hawaii, the Mo'okini temple (*heiau*) originated over 1500 years ago according to the ancient chant (*oli*) passed from the *kahuna nui* of one generation to the next.[6] The *kahunas* committed the genealogical chants to memory, the only way to preserve knowledge of the sacred lineage.[7] King Kamehameha the Great received his birth rites at this same Mo'okini *heiau* in the mid eighteenth century. Scholars of Hawaii as well as many tourists to the Islands know about this sacred historic site in North Kohala, Hawaii.

---

[6] Most archeologists approximate the initial colonization of the Hawaiian Islands in the first centuries after Christ. Noted native anthropologist at the University of California Berkeley, Patrick Kirch dates the Colonization Period 300-600 A.D. See Patrick Kirch and Marshall Sahlins, <u>Anahulu: The Anthropology of History in the Kingdom of Hawaii Vol.Two</u>. Chicago: University of Chicago Press, 1992, p.7, 12-13. Also see University of Aukland archeologist, Geoffrey Irwin, <u>The Prehistoric Exploration and Colonization of the Pacific</u>. Cambridge: Cambridge University Press, 1992, p. 78.

[7] George Hu'eu Sanford Kanahele, <u>Ku Kanaka Stand Tall: A Search for Hawaiian Values</u>. Honolulu: University of Hawaii Press, 1986, p. 58.

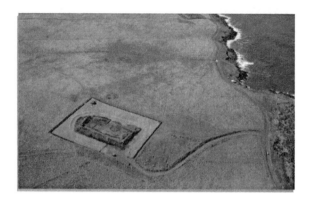

[Aerial View of the Mo'okini Heiau]

Located on the northernmost tip of the Big Island of Hawaii, on the open plain 1000 feet from the ocean, is the enormous Mo'okini Heiau (temple), approximately 280 feet by 140 feet. The construction of the *heiau* allowed open access to the skies; the temple never had a roof.

The east wall was 19.3 feet high, while its thickness was 6 feet at the top and 33.9 feet (including 3.5 feet wide bench on the side) at the base.

The upper surface of the north and south walls was originally of the same width and elevation as that of the east wall, although the bases are much narrower.

The west wall is much like a high platform, being 8.5 feet high, 15 feet wide at the top and 18 feet wide (excluding the bench) at the base.[8]

The birth site of King Kamehameha I (the Great) is down the hill from this *heiau*, and the Mo'okini *kahuna nui* (high priest) officiated at the birth rites for the newly born king.

Again, the contemporary high priestess (*kahuna nui*) is Zita Leimomi Mo'okini Lum.   The name <u>Momi</u> (from **Leimomi**) means rare black pearl in Hawaiian. For Momi to become the seventh female *kahuna nui* of the Mo'okini line (a role usually reserved for men), she must be of the **blood line, chosen** by the *kahuna nui* preceding her and be **temple-trained**.   Uncle Heloke Mo'okini, *kahuna nui* from 1930-1966, chose Momi for this significant role in the Hawaiian religious tradition, and before his death, he performed the *Ha* ritual,[9] transferring the powerful role of *kahuna nui* to his niece after her temple-training and after the death of her father. Momi's father, Dewey Mo'okini, *kahuna nui* from 1966 to 1977, concurred with his brother's choice of his daughter Momi as the next *kahuna nui.*

Momi possesses a distinct mana. *Mana,* a significant Hawaiian word, conveys the meaning of power perceived by the individual and those around the person, but believed to originate in

---

[8.] John F.G. Stokes, Heiau of the Island of Hawaii: A Historic Survey of Native Hawaiian Temple Sites.   Honolulu: Bishop Museum Press, 1991, p. 173 ff.

[9.] Mary Kawena Pukui describes this solemn ritual: "A person about to die expelled his breath into the chosen successor's mouth. With this the *mana* (power) that made him an expert in an art or craft passed directly to one particular person, not to the family in general." Mary Kawena Pukui, E.W. Haertig and Catherine A. Lee, Nana I Ke Kumu (Look to the Source). Vol. I. Honolulu: Hui Hanai, Queen Lili'uokalani Children's Center, 1972, p. 43 ff, 151.

the supernatural. A Hawaiian believer recognizes a mystic quality to the personal magnetism which the unbeliever reduces to a mere human trait.[10]

Many in the Hawaiian Islands and well beyond speak about Momi as *kahuna nui* and as *tutu*, an affectionate term which "refers loosely to a woman of a grandparent generation which is used to mean 'auntie'...a term for an older woman who guides and teaches younger persons."[11]   While Uncle Heloke envisioned opening the Mo'okini *heiau* to the children of Hawaii, he charged Momi with the responsibility of finding a way to modify a *heiau* reserved for the kings and ruling chiefs (*ali'i*) and open it to the children. After much thought and prayer for divine guidance and wisdom (*ike*), in a ceremony sacred to the Hawaiian religious tradition, Momi lifted one powerful *kapu* (taboo, restriction): no longer would human sacrifice to the god Ku occur at the Mo'okini heiau...so that the children could come for guidance, wisdom, prayer, knowledge of themselves in light of the sacred Hawaiian traditions. On a specified date in early November, during a period called *Makahiki*[12] from Hawaii of old, for the last thirty-four years Momi and her docents welcome up to a thousand children to the Mo'okini *heiau*, in which Momi tells the children unequivocally: "I leave you a legacy to your heritage."[13] As *kahuna nui*, Momi describes the focus of her efforts as a "commitment to the children of tomorrow."[14] From 1977 Momi

---

[10.] Pukui,Haertig, Lee, Nana I Ke Kumu, Vol 1, p. 149 ff.

[11.] Ibid., p. 27.

[12.] An ancient festival beginning about the middle of October and lasting about four months with religious festivities and sports and a taboo on war. See Mary Kawena Pukui and Samuel H. Elbert, <u>Hawaiian Dictionary: Hawaiinan-English, English-Hawaiian</u> (Revised and Enlarged Edition). Honolulu: University of Hawaii Press, 1986, p. 225.

[13.] Presentation to the children at the Mo'okini *heiau* on 7 November 2003.

[14.] Personal interview with Zita Leiomomi Mo'okini Lum 5 December

opened the *heiau* to the children of Hawaii; from 1994 to the children of the world. While this Children's Day is the largest event at the *heiau* in a year, periodically Momi welcomes other smaller groups.

[Momi Lum the *kahuna nui*]

Zita is Momi's baptismal name. She is a devout Roman Catholic.[15] Since the arrival of the Catholic missionaries to Hawaii in 1827, the Mo'okini line converted to Catholicism. Momi explains that as Catholics we understand one God with three divine persons: Father, Son and Holy Spirit. Using the Hawaiian religious frame of reference, Momi understands the one God as Io or I and the three divine persons as Kane (Father), Ku (Son) and Lono (Holy Spirit). Momi and those before her in generations since the conversion to Catholicism consider Kanaloa to be Luicifer, but she respects the religion of her elders, her forebears. Not all believers in the Hawaiian religious tradition would find this way of synthesizing the Hawaiian religious and Catholic traditions acceptable.[16]

2003.
  [15.] Patti Cook, <u>Mo'okini *Luakini*:Koki'iki, North Kohala, Hawaii</u>. Honolulu: Mo'okini Luakini, Inc., 1984, p. 2.
  [16.] Not every Hawaiian who cares deeply about his or her heritages would understand these principle Hawaiian gods (*akua*) as Father, Son, Holy Spirit and Lucifer. See Mary Kawena Pukui, E. W. Haertig and Catherine A. Lee, <u>Nana I Ke Kumu (Look to the Source)</u>. Vol. 1. Honolulu:

The primary concern of this author: to accurately present the understanding of Momi Lum as the current *kahuna nui* of the Mo'okini line and all who follow her lead. While Momi states unequivocally that she is a Catholic, she welcomes all to the Mo'okini *heiau* and invites them to pray in whatever way seems right to them. How **ancient** Hawaiians understood the four primary gods can be studied elsewhere.

So, this book will examine how the contemporary Mo'okini Hawaiian religious perspective (as explicated by the *kahuna nui*) compares with contemporary Catholic perspectives (as explicated by this author) in several areas of common concern for someone seeking growth in the spiritual life today. At our time and place in the world, the spirits of many are broken or are breaking in the context of modern life. For more than a few, fresh perspectives can foster and enhance the desire for deeper connection with God, self and others. Even though some may find this comparative approach problematic,[17] hopefully it will broaden awareness for many through comparison and contrast, and motivate thoughtful choices for action.

Hui Hanai, Queen Lili'uokalani Children's Center, 1972, p. 24.

[17.] "Comparisons are odious as the aphorism says partly because they tend to downplay and distort the contrasts...but ultimately the object of all religious ritual overrides history and theology, for it deals with the basic human 'sense of the holy' which is the same everywhere." See George Hu'eu Sanford Kanahele, <u>Ku Kanaka Stand Tall: A Search for Hawaiian Values</u>. Honolulu: University of Hawaii Press, 1986,
p.12 109.

Part One: Retrofitting the Foundation

E hana mua a pa'a ke kahua
Mamua o ke a'o ana aku ia ha'i

Build yourself a firm foundation
Before teaching others.[18]

The word carries noteworthy power in the Hawaiian language. Chants, proverbs, prayers and Hawaiian sayings require the right words. Great care accompanies the choice of words. Dictionaries provide approximate meanings in English, but the fuller resonances can elude us. Sometimes the speaker and listener conjure up double or more connotations, as well as the sentiment with which

---

[18] Mary Kawena Pukui, 'Olelo No'eau: Hawaiian Proverbs and Poetical Sayings. Honolulu: Bishop Museum Press (Special Publication 71), 1983, p. 34, no. 276.

the chant or proverb is voiced or received in a particular time and place.[19]

In light of this Hawaiian saying, we focus attention upon our foundation as a person. We can only offer what we have to give. This is the premise. We do what we know. This being said, usually we have received more than we realize or appropriate fully. If we are open to learning more about these gifts, we can live more fully in ways we could hardly imagine.

Many today experience confusion about their foundational identity. How do we identify ourselves? Where is home base? Many Hawaiians and mainland USA Roman Catholics expend a lot of energy and emotion trying to find their identity. If we do not have a clear identity, then we are lost, wandering. We need to find ways to get home. It can be helpful, though, to acknowledge that we are lost when this is the truth. Then we can look for who and what might enable us to establish or to re-establish the foundation upon which we build.

When sizable earthquakes rock and roll, even foundations of major structures experience the effects. Sometimes the effects are substantial enough to require retrofitting, like happened recently on some major freeways in the San Francisco Bay Area. Without retrofitting, these ways of passing could collapse and then people would be hurt and die. A precarious situation in which the stakes are high.

Many contemporary Hawaiians as well as mainlanders experience home base as shaky. Whether we are parents living with children, single parents, adults who live alone or with others, too

---

[19.] Personal interview with Zita Leimomi Mo'okini Lum 2003.

often we attempt to stand and move, finding the foundation on which we stand giving way. The foundation needs shoring up, retrofitting, to withstand the current earthquakes which rock the foundation.

The symptoms that something is radically wrong: suicide is the second highest killer of young people, 13-30 years of age; clinical depression rates are off the charts; a crippling emotional numbness and *ennui* seem to be spreading; cynicism, seeing reality without hope, runs rampant. Something is radically wrong and if we simply "go with the flow," as the current popular cultural idiom professes, we may well collapse along the way.

According to *kahuna nui* Momi Mo'okini Lum, many contemporary Hawaiians have an unstable identity, shifting in the face of numerous foundational variables.[20] The same could well be said of many mainland USA Catholics. Let us examine some of the underlying causes which rocked the foundation.

Usually ancient Hawaiians had a healthy sense of identity, to use a contemporary way of speaking. They sensed themselves in relationships of significance with the ever-present gods and with the extended family and tribe. These relationships included family members who had died. These relationships served as the foundational focus of their lives, the bedrock.

---

20. Personal interview with Zita Leimomi Mo'okini Lum 2003. Not all Hawaiian thinkers would agree with this assessment. For example, George Kanahele gauges the "emotional and spiritual capacity of contemporary Hawaiians is as high as it has ever been. This partly reflects the increasing improvement of a Hawaiian's overall situation, and especially his sense of identity, for when people feel good about themselves they are much more willing to share with others both themselves and their belongings." See Kanahele, Ku Kanaka Stand Tall, p. 493.

Although not true in most Hawaiian homes today, every home in ancient Hawaii had its own altar (*kuahu*) erected to the family ancestral gods (*'aumakua*); but this factor was only part of a much bigger picture.[21] The gods were everywhere in their experience. For example, "The feast and good times of the Old Hawaiians were not just social good times when people got together and ate and talked and sang and enjoyed themselves. Every feast in the old times followed some religious celebration. There was always a sacred part which came first."[22] Unfortunately, this fundamental relationship with God seems out of focus today in our American atheistic culture, including Hawaii. Contemporary celebrations like Thanksgiving, for instance, provide almost exclusive focus on the social enjoyment of the occasion with little or no explicit awareness of gratitude to God for all we have received. Most of the time, our relationship with God remains tangential at best. We gather for no other purpose that to have a good time. Of course, we do not know that all ancient Hawaiians remembered the sacred character of such gatherings. Perhaps some got distracted by mere repetition of words and gestures, but "the fact remains that these feasts had their religious side which, if it were truly remembered, was very solemn and had great significance."[23]

Ancient Hawaiians anchored themselves in relationship with the major gods (*akua*: I or Io, Kane, Ku, Lono and Kanaloa)[24] and they invoked these for major events and major causes, sometimes

---

[21.] E.S. Craighill Handy et al., <u>Ancient Hawaiian Civilization</u>. Rutland, VT: Charles E. Tuttle Co Publishers, 1965, p. 47.

[22.] Ibid., p. 61.

[23.] Ibid., p. 67.

[24.] Like in Greek mythology, the *akuas* combined both supernatural qualities along with many natural, human frailties. For example, "the *akuas* could be vengeful, helpful or destructive, wise or capricious. This is in direct contrast to the Christian concept of all good and all evil." See Pukui, Haertig and Lee, <u>Nana I Ke Kumu (Look to the Source)</u>, Vol. 1, p. 23.

needing the assistance of priests (*kahunas*). These greater gods had public temples (*heiaus*), of which the Mo'okini *heiau* dedicated to the god Ku is of the highest order.[25] Hawaiians of old called on their personal ancestral gods (*'aumakuas*) within daily life, finding them more approachable.[26]   No matter what the time of year, each kind of work or play–even sports–had a god with whom the ancient Hawaiian would relate. Is this relationship with God a substantial part of the foundational structure of our lives?

Today many of us in our part of the world either never experienced a foundational relationship with God or we got distracted along the way with many other concerns, choosing to let the connection with God wane and become anemic. Is God the homing point of all our relationships?

In ancient Hawaii the immediate family (*'ohana*)[27] formed a sturdy foundation as well. The *'ohana* used to include parents and any relation of the parental generation (*makuas*), grandparents (*kupunas*), children (*keikis*) and ancestral gods (*'aumakuas*).[28] These immortal relatives of the Hawaiian family of old were gods as well. "As gods and relatives in one, they give us strength when we are weak, warning when danger threatens, guidance in our bewilderment, and inspiration in our arts. They are equally our judges, hearing our words and watching our actions, reprimanding us

---

[25.] Handy, <u>Ancient Hawaiian Civilization</u>, p. 47.

[26.] Pukui, Haertig and Lee, <u>Nana I Ke Kumu (Look to the Source)</u>, Vol 1, p. 24. Also they refer to a convenient reference listing of Hawaiian gods in <u>The New Hawaiian Dictionary</u> by Mrs. Pukui and Dr. Samuel H. Elbert, published in 1971.

[27.] *'Oha* literally means a sprout or off-shoots of the taro plant, the staple of ancient Hawaiian life. See Craighill and Pukui, <u>The Polynesian Family System</u>, p. 3.

[28.] Pukui, Haertig and Lee, <u>Nana I Ke Kumu (Look to the Source)</u>, Vol 1, p. 167.

for our error and punishing us for blatant offense...these are our spiritual parents."[29]   The 'aumakua could "pass on" prayers to the akua, as well as be a "spiritual go-between."[30]   Hawaiians of old could commune with the 'aumakua throughout the day and throughout life. Even death lost its sting to the one who believed "his soul will be warmly received and safely guided by his 'aumakua."[31] As a Catholic today, kahuna nui Momi Mo'okini Lum understands these beloved 'aumakua as part of the Communion of the Saints, those who have gone before us in the faith and live now with God and accompanying us, providing all those wonderful aforementioned ways of caring for us.[32]

The ancient Hawaiians believed in kino lau, that is, the gods could and sometimes would manifest themselves in multiple "forms as sharks, owls, mudhens, caterpillars, lizards, eels, and even rocks and plants."[33] To the Hawaiian of old, this revered portion of the family could show up at any time. They were with you, part of the family life.

Even though men and woman of the family ('ohana) ate separately in ancient Hawaii,[34] families did pray and eat together regularly. The notion of "dine and dash" or of eating alone on a regular basis would not exist in old Hawaii. The gathering for a meal nourished the body, but also regularly fed the relationships in ways our contemporary individualism feeds a growing sense of

---

29. Ibid., p. 35.

30. Ibid.

31. Ibid., p. 82.

32. Personal interview with Zita Leimomi Mo'okini Lum 18 August 2003.

33. Kanahele, Ku Kanaka Stand Tall, p. 85.

34. Actually little boys also ate with the women until after the ceremony which marked their entry into manhood. See Pukui, Haertig and Lee, Nana I Ke Kumu (Look to the Source), Vol 1, p. 7.

isolation and rocks the foundation of the family. How many of us eat alone on a regular basis? As individuals we can lose a sense of being part of the lives of others and of their being a foundational part of ours. This destabilizes our sense of ourselves–even as an individual, but also as being part of the group. We cannot "talk story" alone. "Everything relating to the individual is within the matrix of *'ohana*. An individual alone is unthinkable in the context of the Hawaiian relationship."[35] The fact that there was no word for <u>welcome</u> in the language may well have meant that for Hawaiians this was such a natural part of life that they had no need for a word to define it. Like the "Inuit (Eskimos) have many words to describe certain types of snowfall but they have no word for snowfall itself."[36]

In contemporary times in Hawaii and for many Catholics in mainland USA, these foundational relationships with God and family and even with others beyond the extended family often seem tenuous. Other concerns compete for time and energy. Work usually gets the lion's share of the prime time and energy. Often we give God and family what remains, left-overs. We can all survive on left-overs for a while, but after a while they get old. A steady diet of left-overs and we could find ourselves in anemic relationships, the foundations of which will be tested.

Another variable which rocks the foundation of the contemporary person: confusing need and greed. In ancient Hawaii many were content with what they had. The cultural customs included sharing whatever they had, even with strangers.[37]

---

[35] Handy and Pukui, <u>The Polynesian Family System</u>, p. 75.
[36] Office of Hawaiian Affairs, <u>Ho'okipa: Hawaiian Hospitality</u>. Honolulu: Office of Hawaiian Affairs, 1988, p. 5.
[37] Personal interview with Zita Leimomi Mo'okini Lum 12 November 2003.

Today in Hawaii and mainland USA we rarely seem to have <u>enough</u>. Many of us slip into craving more power, prestige, money and the things it buys. If our focus becomes building up and protecting all that we have, then this can blur a focus on a sharing what we have and foster a preoccupation with getting more, better, newer, faster, smaller, bigger, etc. The more gifts for us to carry, the harder it is to carry them with a measure of freedom. We can get distracted by the things themselves. As Jesus said, it is harder for a person with a lot to find the kingdom of God than to get a camel through the eye of the needle.[38] The grass can seem greener on the other side and erode a sense of contentment with who we are and what we have. We might even lose the sense of being loved and loveable for who we **are** and not for what we **have**. Our academic degrees or professional status do not form the foundation for what makes us loveable. Neither do our salaries, cars, houses, vacations, toys (high-tech or not), etc. But in our part of the world at this time, we can mistakenly imagine that we NEED these to establish our worth and self-respect, not to mention the respect of others. Even without realizing it, the pervasive consumerism can skew our vision. We can forget and lose the sense that we are loved for who we are, not for what we have. We could fall into the prevailing cultural flow which seduces us into an insatiable desire for more. And not knowing that these forces affect us, leaves us floundering in ignorance. This not only perpetuates an unhealthy situation, but also can cause the foundation to deteriorate further.

God is know-able; we can develop a relationship with God which forms the foundation of our lives. Hawaiians of old did this; followers of Jesus have done this. Like Hawaiians of old, we too can reference our lives toward those who have gone before us in faith. High priestess Momi Mo'okini Lum understands 'aumakuas

---

[38.] Mark 10:17-30.

and other minor gods of Hawaii as part of the Communion of the Saints.[39]   All too often today we can imagine ourselves as floundering aimlessly without relational rudders to guide us. We need to find something, someone to grab onto, especially when turbulence rocks our world. Look how the country reacted when the terrorism of 9/11 occurred.

In a section of his book which describes the "ghost of inferiority," George Kanahele states that this ghost lurks in the minds of many Hawaiians. "...you have no solid foundation. So you flounder around and you cannot find a place for yourself."[40]

In a recent comedy-drama entitled "It Runs In the Family," Kirk and Mike Douglas (father and son in life and in the movie) demonstrate how for generations the family has wrestled with patterns of relating which left deformmative influences. Finally Kirk Douglas recognizes the destructive pattern, and rather than simply acquiesce and succumb to repeating the same mistakes of the past, he chooses for himself and for his son and his grandson...to change.

I ka nana no a 'ike.
By observing, one learns.[41]

Without observing and learning from our past, we have no future.   Former Big Island state senator and president of the Kamehameha Schools/Bernice Pauahi Bishop Estate's board of trustees, Richard Ka'ilihiwa Lyman offered his thoughts on the matter: "We were led to believe that we could not know who we were until we knew who and where we had been. How could we

---

[39.] Personal interview with Zita Leimomi Mo'okini Lum 15 September 2003.

[40.] Kanahele, Ku Kanaka Stand Tall, p. 21-22.

[41.] Pukui, 'Olelo: Hawaiian Proverbs, p. 129, no. 1186.

learn from the past if we knew nothing about it? It was also agreed by most educators that those who did not learn history were forced to re-experience the mistakes of the past...we can better understand ourselves and develop our identity, get rid of our alienations, only if we knew of our past."[42]

Surely the way we were raised in the past influences us. Observing these influences and learning more about how they tend to move us can yield awareness of our patterns. We can choose to move further into or to back away from ways of relating which form (or deform) our foundation. Sometimes we need help to do this.

Who is in control of our time? Ultimately, God is. Within limits we can choose to structure our time in such a way that it reflects the relational priorities we want. Structure is our friend or it can become such a friend if it enables us to solidify the foundational relationships we want to ground our lives. Talk alone will not yield life which satisfies and lasts, as Jesus reminded us.[43] And passivity always remains a tempting alternative.

Explore and discover what opens wider horizons. Go back to basics, like a child.[44] Shore up our relationship with Jesus. "You form a building which rises on the foundation of the apostles and the prophets, with Christ Jesus himself as the capstone. Through him the whole structure is fitted together and takes shape as a holy temple in the Lord; in him you are being built into this temple, to become a dwelling place for God in the Spirit."[45]

[42.] Richard Ka'ilihiwa Lyman, _Mea Ho'omana: Thoughts_. Honolulu, The Estate of Richard Lyman, 1995, p. 10.
[43.] Matthew 7:21.
[44.] Luke 10: 21.
[45.] Ephesians 2: 19-22.

We can take initiative to re-establish the foundation of our day. We can choose to spend quality time, take time "off the top," to be with God. We can choose to ask others to pray with us–both in a more structured place like a church and in less formal settings, e.g., around a dinner table. The old adage continues to bear significance: the family that prays together stays together. We can give each other our faith if we choose to do so. It will affect our relationships.

Ka manu ka'upu halo 'ale o
ka moana.

The *ka'upu*, the bird that
observes the ocean.
(Said of a careful observer).[46]

We can look for **mentors** to observe. We can learn from mentors of all ages. The incoming president of the North American Academy of Liturgy during her vice presidential address at the 2003 annual meeting described how her young child taught her some of the most significant lessons of her life. For example, she taught her how to see again with awe and wonder.

We can choose others with whom to break bread and share a meal. "...still much of the spirit of old Hawaii lives when usually dozens of family members, friends and neighbors get together to provide and prepare food, in mutual helpfulness known as *kokua* or *laulima* (many hands). And certainly in the eating, drinking, singing and talking together, the ties of man to fellow man are strengthened in the mutual regard and love summed up as *aloha*."[47]

[46.] Pukui, *'Olelo*: Hawaiian Proverbs, p. 160, no. 1479.
[47.] Pukui, Haertig and Lee, Nana I Ke Kumu (Look to the Source), Vol 1, p. 3.

We can learn from mentors how to speak about matters of our interior life, which casual acquaintances would never know. For example, with acquaintances we would not usually discuss what scares us, what inspires us, what hurts us, what gives us hope, etc. We reserve these matters for those particularly close to us–those we have found competent, trustworthy and genuinely love us. An example of entrusting those closest to us with our inner life would be the *ho'oponopono* ritual. This ritual of ancient Hawaii was a way to maintain and to restore good relations. One of the forms of *ho'oponopono* focused on the family. The immediate family "set things right through prayer, discussion, confession, repentance and mutual restitution and forgiveness."[48]

This way of Hawaiian families being together continued after the missionaries came. For example, at the end of the last century Mary Kawena Pukui lauded the helpfulness of the *ho'oponopono*: "I took part in *ho'oponopono* myself for 47 years, from semi-Christian to Christian times. And whether my *'ohana* (family) prayed to *'aumakua* (ancestral gods) or to God, the whole idea of *ho'oponopono* was the same. Everyone of us searched his heart for hard feelings against one another. Before God and with his help, we forgave and were forgiven, thrashing out every grudge, peeve or resentment among us."[49] We can learn to talk about and listen to and pray about more of what matters–certainly more than the superficial dribble of so-called reality TV, sports, weather, etc.

Just like Hawaiians of old, we too may need help to learn how to commune on deeper interior levels. For example, in the *ho'oponopono* ritual, a knowledgeable leader helped the family members to share their interior lives. "A successful *ho'oponopono*

[48.] Ibid., p 60.
[49.] Ibid., p. 61.

was not mere emotional catharsis. Hawaiians seemed to know that neither a crying jag nor a shouting match solves a problem...the *ho'oponopono* provision that participants talk about anger to the leader rather than hurling the maledictions at each other was a wise one."[50] Clearly this kind of sharing about tender and painful matters of the interior life required a magnanimity of heart all the way around. "Both must *kala* (to release, untie, unbind, let go). Each must release himself and the other of the deed (wrong), and the recriminations, remorse, grudges, guilts and embarrassments the deed caused. Both must 'let go of the chord,' freeing each other completely, mutually and permanently."[51]

We can look for **things** which spark our attention and widen our horizon. For example, music calls many of us beyond the mundane and cerebral. The style of music can vary for the individual. For some of us certain types of Hawaiian music enable a sense of "more than meets the eye," soothes the soul, inspires and motivates to action. For others Blues, Gospel, Gregorian Chant, Jazz, Classical. Rainbows and waterfalls and clouds and snow can free us when we become careful observers, calling us to realms beyond the superficial. Writing for some of us–in a journal, in a letter, in prose and poetry–can open resevoirs of experience and reflection unknown to the less observant among us.

As in many cultures of the past, including the Hawaiian, both feasting and fasting can lessen outside influences which distract us. We can be more aware of inner thoughts and can be more likely to address them and to express them. With less distractions and if we pay attention, we can learn more about our deeper wishes, urges, loves, fears, conflicts, including volatile inner matter we buried.[52]

---

[50] Ibid., p. 68.
[51] Ibid., p. 75.
[52] Ibid., p. 5.

We can look for rituals which make sense to us. When speaking about the value of ritual, George Kanahele states that "it is probably the most complete and dynamic form of communication, for it involves words, symbols, sounds, colors, smells, touchings, tastings, rhythms, visualizations, space-and-time settings–every conceivable teaching aid...repetition is *mater studiorum* (mother of learning); by nature ritual repeats."[53] Of course, we must include enough variety and change to achieve a deeper understanding and sense of the spiritual. Stale repetition bores and over-done ritual draws attention to itself. The point is to explore what opens wider horizons and to play with new possibilities which free the spirit within and among us. We can worship God through ritual ways which open us to graced insight about how to take the next best step toward thriving and not merely surviving.

We can look for **places** to open up and to explore our interior life, even where it feels like Pandora's Box within us. The place may be at the waterfront, on a mountain peak, on top of a skyscraper, in a woods, in a meadow under the shade of an oak tree. It may be a *heiau* or a church. God is everywhere. For us to spend quality time together is the point. Identify several places we can go <u>be</u> and not need to <u>do</u> anything. If we have ever been in love, we know the experience of how good it can be just to be together–what we do does not matter so much. We can tell God what we want, why we want it, why we think he should give it to us; but then we need to sit and wait.[54] We all need places which become significant to us as "holy ground," where we meet God, ourselves and others on a regular basis.

O ke kahua mamua, mahope ke kukulu.

---

53. Kanahele, <u>Ku Kanaka Stand Tall,</u> p. 109.
54. Personal interview with Zita Leimomi Mo'okini Lum 3 December 2003.

The site first, and then the building.
(Learn all you can, then practice).[55]

Then we need to practice what we observed and learned. Practice seeing what meets the eye and, paradoxically, we will see more than meets the eye. As we slow down and sit with our experience, God will open ways as the clutter settles. We will hear silence and sounds we missed before, and begin to notice the cacophony in the world around us and sometimes within us. As we practice quieting down with the Lord, each other and even by ourselves, more often we will find parts of ourselves we lost or never knew. God reveals more of the truth to us as we acknowledge and accept what is real. Finding out more about who we are and where we come from can liberate us toward where we want to go, yielding a peace the world cannot know.

Habits cultivate character–good ones and bad ones. Self-direction alone often provides an inadequate center board for the human journey. Dividends will emerge if we practice the childlike learning of the patterns we observe from mentors, things and places; these will deepen and broaden our interior life. Lo and behold, we will change and discover ourselves drawn to choose to unite more with God and others and to solidify these foundational relationships in our lives. The quantity and especially the quality of these connections will form the foundation on which we operate.

This human journey of ours is not a dress rehearsal. This is not the "practice round." This is our one human lifetime. The gifts we receive are precious and fragile, and they do not keep. Our resources have limits. Our choices consequences. All the more

---

[55.] Pukui, *'Olelo: Hawaiian Proverbs*, p. 268, no. 2459.

reason to practice anchoring in the relationships which mean the most.

Part Two: Finding God in All Things

Ka honua nui a Kane i ho'inana
a 'ahu kinohinohi.

Kane was the god of life
and fresh water.[56]

Are we looking for God? Are we just looking out for self, old No. 1? A simplistic answer would reduce the difficulty of the diagnosis and treatment. Unfortunately the situation remains more complicated by a blend.

At a time and place in the world which often seeks pleasure, power and fame, why does it surprise us that so many of us are frequently self-centered rather than God-centered? Is it any wonder that we discover little or nothing that is sacred? How often we lament the lack of respect for others evidenced in the growing violence of our USA culture. The graffiti, the verbal abuse given to authority figures–whether parents, teachers, police, elders, etc., the

---

[56.] Pukui, *'Olelo*: Proverbs, p. 143, no.1316.

"acting out" of anger on the road and in the air, so much of popular music and movies. Of course these examples merely touch the surface of the physical abuse in our culture, culminating in the horrendous violent crime statistics. Why does all this lack of respect for others surprise us when there seems to be a deteriorating respect for self—a self-respect no longer anchored in finding God? If we look out for God and find God's love for us reflected all over, how could we not respect ourselves and other persons, places and things which God created?

> *E hahai ana no ke kolekole i*
> *kahi nui a ka wahie, a e hahai*
> *ana no ke 'ino i kahi nui o Kapa'akai.*

> Underdone meat follows along
> even where wood is plentiful,
> and decomposition follows along
> even where much salt is found.
> [Even where good is found, evil creeps in].[57]

Whether we understand our clay feet through this ancient Hawaiian metaphor of cooking or curing of meat in this proverb, of course we are human. Our prisms are cracked. We look out into the world within us and around us through a cracked lens. Our vision is skewed. While true, this human vision is all we have, and God can help us mend the cracks, so that we grow in our ability to find God, everywhere.

Ancient Hawaiian sources reveal a spiritual vision in the culture. The belief that the spiritual permeated persons, places and things constituted part of the cultural frame of reference. It was a

---

[57.] Ibid., p. 34, no. 271.

"given" at that time and place. Multiple sources such as Drs. Handy and Pukui describe how the Hawaiian of old lived alert to the relationship with the divine around him. What many from other times and places would call inanimate could be seen by ancient Hawaiians as forms assumed by individual spirits to whom they were related.[58] These people could find God. Ironically and offensively, some literature from early Christian explorers and settlers referred to these same Hawaiians as pagans and savages, offering their "heathen prayers."[59]

To the Hawaiian of old, supernatural beings pervaded the universe. Every occupation or situation had some god, spiritual entity to call upon for aid, protection, gratitude, etc.[60] A common invocation to the supernatural reveals their spiritual view of the world:

"E ho'oulu ana ikini o ke akua,
Ka lehu o ke akua, ka mano o ke akua.

Invoke we now the 40,000 gods,
the 400,000 gods, the 4,000 gods."[61]

---

[58]. E.S. Craighill Handy and Mary Kawena Pukui, The Polynesian Family System in Ka-'u, Hawaii. Wellington, N.Z.: The Polynesian Society, Inc., 1958, p. 27.
[59]. Abraham Fornander, Hawaiian Antiquities and Folklore: Vol. VII, No. 1. Honolulu, Bishop Museum Press, 1919, p. 46.
[60]. J. Halley Cox and William H. Davenport, Hawaiian Sculpture. Honolulu: The University of Hawaii Press, 1974, p. 21.
[61]. Kanahele, Ku Kanaka Stand Tall, p. 70. Also see David Malo, Hawaiian Antiquities (Moolelo Hawaii). Honolulu: Bernice P. Bishop Museum Press, 1951, p. 85.

When Hawaiians of old prayed, they added these words to their prayer. No one knew the exact number of the gods. This provided a figurative expression about the Hawaiian pantheon.

In ancient Hawaii, each major god handled areas of responsibility. A variety of epithets associated with each god designated aspects of the god's responsibility.

Kane - "Countless are his forms; he is Kane...in the whirlwind...the-great-wind...the-little-wind...the peaceful breezes...in the rainbow...of many types of clouds... in-the-heavenly star...in-the-great-outpouring-of-water...in-the-little-outpouring-of-water...of the mountain...of the precipice...the-out-cropping-stone... in the sea...coral of many sorts...fresh water for irrigation."[62]

"Life-giving-one...god-of-the-shooting-herb...the-water-of-eternal-life."[63]

Ku - "adzing-out-the-canoe...of-fishing...of-war...the-supreme-one...the-snatcher-of-islands."[64]...of the stste...of the rulers and...source of wisdom and guidance."[65]

Lono- "Of the blue heavens, let the crops flourish in this land...cared for maturation, forgiveness, healing, other life-giving aspects."[66]

[62.] Handy and Pukui, The Polynesian Family System, p. 34.

[63.] Cox and Davenport, Hawaiian Sculpture, p. 16.

[64.] Ibid.

[65.] Lecture at the University of Hawaii by Zita Leimomi Mo'okini Lum, April, 1975, p. 39.

[66.] Ibid.

"...the heaven was sacred to Lono (the Makahiki god)...the thunder...the earth... life...the hills...the mountains...the ocean...the raging surf...the family...the sailing canoe..."[67]
"Ku was the god of the chiefs, but Lono was the god of the people. His temples were built 'no ke ola o ka 'aina," so that the land might live. Lono was a god of compassion who brought rainfall and nourishment to the land. In this Makahiki chant, which celebrates growth and abundance, Lono is entreated to 'shake out a net full of food...' "[68]

Kanaloa Of the ocean...below the earth."[69] In general, the ancient Hawaiian viewed "the worth of religion corresponds to its ability to make life easier, richer, better, or happier not just for the soul, but the body as well."[70] The spiritual perspective permeated all of life. For example, "Malo wrote that 'when the people and the priests saw that the services of the *luakini* (a temple, the highest order of *heiau*) were well-conducted, they began to have confidence in the stability of the government."[71] Like all Polynesians, the Hawaiians believed in the existence of a spiritual power they called *mana*. "Hawaiians believed that all things–'animate and inanimate, objects and creatures'–are inter-related by the all-pervading creative force: *mana*, the divine power of the gods."[72] And the Hawaiians of old willingly accommodated many gods, "particularly any new gods that appeared to possess more *mana* than did the old ones."[73]

---

[67] Fornander, Hawaiian Antiquities, p. 40.

[68] Malo, Hawaiian Antiquities (Moolelo Hawaii), p. 177.

[69] Personal interview with Zita Leimomi Mo'okini Lum, 2 January 2004

[70] Kanahele, Ku Kanaka Stand Tall, p. 112.

[71] Ibid., p. 113.

[72] Ibid., p. 96.

[73] Ibid., p. 76.

In the first line of his poem "God's Grandeur," the nineteenth century Jesuit poet Gerard Manley Hopkins wrote: "The world is charged with the grandeur of God."[74] Can we not find this God in the world charged with God's grandeur? "Nothing was done in ancient Hawaii without acknowledging the presence and power of the gods and goddesses. There was no word for religion in the ancient days; the entirety of life was religious."[75] This being said, what we in contemporary USA describe as religion played a pivotal role in ancient Hawaii. "Religion was the central authority of early Hawaiian society...No activity of any consequence lay outside the influence of the *kahuna* (priest), the *kapu* (sacred regulations) they pronounced, the rituals, symbols, and myths of religion. It dictated the content, tempo, direction, and density of the life of every man, woman, and child. Religion enveloped nearly everything–the hula and *mele* (song), wars and games, planting and harvesting, healing and dying, dreaming and prophesying, and procreating. Life and religion were inseparably one."[76]

Mary Kawena Pukui referred to how Hawaiians experienced God in their world when she stated: "There are many references to supernatural or mystic occurrences...Hawaiian life and thought cannot be understood without knowing about them."[77] In the Hawaiian culture of old "human affairs and mystical-religious concerns were often indivisible."[78] To exemplify the contrast between our secular contemporary way of obtaining medicine as a

---

[74.] Oscar Williams, ed., <u>A Pocket Book of Modern Verse</u> (Revised Edition). Washington Square Press, p. 135.

[75.] M.J. Harden, <u>Voices of Wisdom: Hawaiian Elders Speak</u>. Kula, HI: Aka Press, 1999,p. 41.

[76.] Kanahele, Ku Kanaka Stand Tall, p. 32.

[77.] <u>Ibid</u>, p. 43.

[78.] Pukui, Haertig and Lee, <u>Nana I Ke Kumu (Look to the Source)</u>, Vol 1, p.47.

mundane task and the ancient Hawaiian approach, Drs. Pukui, Haertig and Lee describe how Hawaiians of old gathered "curative plants ritually, plucking five with the right hand and praying to the god Ku, then five with the left hand as he prayed to the goddess Hina. And so his errand became equally a religious rite."[79] Phycologist and ethnobotonist at the University of Hawaii, Dr. Isabella Aiona Abbott noted that "the role plants played in the lives of the ancients is all tied to religion...Hawaiian use and understanding of plants was thoroughly and profoundly religious. This was due to their belief that maintaining a right relationship with the gods and the earth is humanity's basic spiritual challenge."[80]

Who do we think we are that we do not need God? Whose world is this? A tempting alternative these days: to say it is ours...it's all about us. Talk about self-centered! Some find God coming out of their mouths when they bump into an experience in which they feel out of control. For example, the same politicians who usually emphasize the separation of church and state and that religion is a private matter, when faced with the sudden and devastating terrorism of 911, assembled on the steps of the Capitol in Washington, D.C., to sing a prayer: "God, Bless America." When someone gets startled by an unexpected automobile accident or illness, the person may exclaim, "Oh God..." They may even risk entering a church or into an honest conversation with a person of faith, and finding God within this situation beyond their control. Often we live with this illusion that we are in control. We need to wake up from this fantasy and live in the real world which is more mysterious and filled with the grandeur of God, in ways we hardly imagine these days.

---

79. Ibid.
80. M.J. Harden, Voices of Wisdom, p. 28.

God gives us life and all that we have within us and around us. If we open our minds and our hearts and our senses to seek God, we will find God in the world charged with God's grandeur, even if the world "wears man's smudge and shares man's smell."[81] Let us examine some examples of how Hawaiians of old were finding God in all things.

---

[81]. Gerard Manley Hopkins, "God's Grandeur."

Time

Indigenous Hawaiians approached their lives with a cultural sense that their time was precious and sacred. "The moon calendar was based on spiritual beliefs. Several days of every twenty-eight day moon cycle were devoted to certain gods, and these days were considered times for rest and renewal–no planting, no fishing, only play, celebration and religious ritual."[82] The Hawaiians of old made *kapu* (sacred restrictions) the last three months of the year called *Makahiki*. There would be no war, and at first the people would eat no pork, coconut, fish, fresh foods (*'i'o*); and then, after the *kahuna* (priest) consecrated these good gifts to the god of the *Makahiki* (*Lono*), he would declare them free (*noa*) for all to share.[83] In addition, Hawaiians of old prayed before and after anything they did, e.g., a meal, planting, fishing, going to bed, etc. Each day high noon was a time when ancient Hawaiians dropped their plows or whatever their activities and prayed.[84]

For many in the contemporary USA culture, driven by its secular and work-oriented forces, such a frame of reference might seem unthinkable, impractical even for those of us who claim to be spiritual. To orient ourselves as the Hawaiians of old, we would need to choose time for equivalent sacred activities. For many of us, it is not simple to reserve an hour even once a week for public worship. If we would try to mark a significant amount of our time with some special way of orienting it to God, no doubt we would experience ourselves swimming up-stream. We will feel resistance

---

[82.] M.J. Harden, Voices of Wisdom, p. 20.

[83.] Samuel Manaiakalani Kamakau, *Ka Po'e Kahiko*: The People of Old. Honolulu: The Bishop Museum Press, 1987, p. 27.

[84.] Personal interview with Zita Leimomi Mo'okini Lum 2 January 2004.

from within as well as without because the predominant flow will be going in other directions. Yet such counter-cultural choices provide us with a new lens with which to look for God. What a find this would be.

Birth

When experiencing the birth of a new child, the parents viewed this significant event with eyes of the spirit. Samuel Manaiakalani Kamakau describes the indigenous religious ritual: "In ancient days, when a male child was born he was taken immediately to the *mua* (men's eating house and family 'chapel') to be consecrated, *ho'ola'a*, to the gods."[85]

Meals

The eating of a meal provided a regular meeting ground between people and God. Finding God in a meal setting would have been assumed in the indigenous culture of Hawaii. In explicating their understanding of a feast (*'aha'aina*) which was part of forgiving before Christianity, Drs. Pukui, Haertig and Lee state that "food, often scarce, was precious. What was precious was symbolically offered to the gods...man felt closer to his fellow man when the *opu* (belly) was being filled...would not man and god feel a warm rapport if they ate together?

It seemed so. For the feasts of old Hawaii–and often ordinary meals as well–carried a feeling of eating with and communicating with the gods. They went beyond a ritual offering of the spiritual essence (*aka*) of the food. The god or gods were not offered their portion and then mentally retired to the shelves. A sense of their presence remained throughout the eating. The gap

---

[85.] Kamakau, *Ka Po'e Kahiko: The People of Old*, p. 27.

between man and gods was indeed narrowed, and the gods were thought more receptive to mortal requests for help or forgiveness."[86]

How often do we find God while eating a meal–an ordinary meal or a special celebration like Christmas or Easter or a birthday? Observing the absence of this spiritual awareness and practice in contemporary Hawaii, Drs. Pukui, Haertig and Lee note that "today the gods are rarely present at the feast and the 'aha'aina (feast of forgiving) as a religious observance has almost disappeared...feasting today is usually a purely human affair...the symbolism of the food is usually forgotten."[87] This does not need to be the case.

As red-blooded Americans we tend to soak up the best and the worst of our cultural context, including its secularity and frenetic pace. We can reprioritize and learn from the values of ancient Hawaiians. "So important was *ai* (eating, food) that the gods were ritually fed, and feasting was a religious as well as a social rite."[88] If we do not stop and think twice (re-flect) about our common experience of a meal, we will probably get caught in the prevailing cultural flow and likely not find God. Uncritically "going with the flow" will cause us to lose our relationship with God in ways which make a difference in this world.

Rain

In ancient Hawaii, rain could become a revelation of God. Abraham Fornander recounts his experience of the Hawaiians: "The pig was taken by the priest and offered to the deity with the prayer

---

[86] Pukui, Haertig and Lee, <u>Nana I Ke Kumu (Look to the Source)</u>, Vol 1, p. 1.

[87] Ibid., p. 2.

[88] Ibid., p. 6.

E ke akua, eia ka puaa la e ola i ko pulapula,
A haule iho la ka ua

O God, here is the pig; give thou health (life) to your
offspring and descendants.
Then rain fell (in answer)."[89]

Rainbow

The rainbow provided another avenue to find God:

"*Kau ka 'onohi ali'i i luna.*
The royal eyes above

[A rainbow–a sign that the gods are watching the chiefs–is now
visible.]"[90]

[89.] Fornander, Hawaiian Antiquities, p. 4.

Fish

The Hawaiians of old found fish to be sacred, somewhere to find God:

> *"Auwe mai ana ia'u ka manu i kakio*
> *A Kane i mahi*
> *E mahi mai la o Kikau o Hana.*
> *Kau mai ka oopu ko Waikolu,*
> *E hoi ana wau e ai;*
> *He kala ka'u ia, i ai ai au a maona,*
> *Uwe he ia paia na kuu akua*

> The birds are calling me from the kakio (pattern of flying)
> Which Kane (god) cultivated
> Tilled by Kikau (person) of Hana (place).
> During the *oopu* (fish) season of Waikolu (place)
> I am going home to eat;
> *Kala* is the fish I will eat until satisfied,
> It is the fish sacred to my god; alas!"[91]

Bamboo

An ancient Hawaiian could find God in bamboo. The *kahuna* (priest) uttered this prayer before using the bamboo for the cutting of the foreskin, what we call circumcision:

[90.] Pukui, <u>'Olelo: Proverbs</u>, p. 174, no. 1614.

[91.] Fornander, <u>Hawaiian Antiquities</u>, p. 48.

"Bring the bamboo from Ho-mai-ka-'ohe
Here is the small-leafed bamboo of Kane (god)
Cut now the foreskin
It is divided!"[92]

Procreation, Genetalia

Hawaiians of old viewed procreation and genetalia as sacred parts of life. These embodied blessings of the gods without thought of immodesty. A chant for the sacredness of the genetalia revealed more than poems of praise.[93]

The **sunset** opened vistas for finding God.

"...a Kilele au a Kihoa
He ka kiki, he Kane kiki, he wahine kiki

[92.] Ibid., p. 95.
[93.] Handy and Pukui, The Polynesian Family System, p. 93.

Keiki kiki, ipukai kiki, o hooehu kiki
He hookiki kiki e Lono, o!

"...To Kilele and on to Kihoa
[where] the vines are vigorous, the men energetic, the
women active,
The children sprightly, [the] food vessels supplied,
the red glow intense. Such red glow being caused by
Lono, Oh!"[94]

Finding God throughout nature appears in much of the literature about ancient Hawaii. The aforementioned examples hardly exhaust the points of contact with the gods. "*Wai* (fresh water), salt, fire, height, *ao* (light), gourd, color, pig and other animals and plants convey symbolic meanings which refer to the relationship with God, the sacred."[95]

[94.] Fornander, Hawaiian Antiquities, p. 46.
[95.] Kanahele, Ku Kanaka Stand Tall, p. 47.

Procession

The procession can reveal the presence of the divine as well.

> "...*ka iluna ke ala eKane, Maueleka!*
> *O mai ko luna 'la Maueleka*
> *E aha ana Maueleka*
> *Maaweawe, maakahikahi, a ke kuina*
> *I ka hele ana a Kane.*

> ...the procession, O Kane, marches upward.
> The heavens recognize the procession;...
> Sacred is the procession marching past...
> Slowly moving and singly is the going.
> O Kane, grant us life."[96]

---

96. Fornander, <u>Hawaiian Antiquities</u>, p. 52.

Song and Dance

Hawaiians of old loved their song (*mele*) and dance (*hula*) and both became revelatory of God.[97] "The hula, in days of old, was a sacred dance in honor of the '*aumakuas* (ancestral gods) and *akuas* (major gods)."[98] Many weeks of preparatory training preceded a performance before the king. The performers followed a special diet. Strict *kapus* (sacred regulations) accompanied the training period until they learned all the songs and dances. Then the time arrived for consecrating the singers and dancers. The teacher (*kumu hula*) slaughtered a young pig, which was consecrated to the *akua* (god) of hula. Afterwards each performer ate a little portion of that pig.[99] This ritual sharing of consecrated food provided a meeting ground with God.

A *kumu hula* (hula teacher) for over fifty years, Winona Beamer describes how chant tells the story and the hula sets it in motion. "In hula, the dancers become one with everything in nature. They bent, swayed and gestured, moving in countless ways to tell countless stories, most of which had deep meanings. Behind these graceful, expressive, sometimes dignified and sometimes earthy dances, lay years of study, meditation and prayer."[100]

George Kanahele contrasts this sacred approach to song and dance with the secularism of our time and place. "Nowadays most people automatically think of hula as pure entertainment, pleasing to look at and occasionally provocative, but not as a holy rite or as an

---

97. Handy and Pukui, <u>Polynesian Family System</u>, p. 83.

98. Handy, <u>Ancient Hawaiian Civilization</u>, p. 62.

99. Ibid. "As with the priestly sacrificer and the observing participants in a temple rite, hula dancers too had to be consecrated before their ritual performance." See Kanahele, <u>Ku Kanaka Stand Tall</u>, p. 131.

100. Harden, <u>Voices of Wisdom</u>, p. 98.

integral part of a religious service. In Hawaii of old, the dance began as a religious ritual...but in time it 'degenerated' into folk dance...usually only as a profane vestige of what once was sacred."[101]

The transformative power (*mana*) in the hula of old Hawaii enabled the performer and those witnessing the performance an opportunity to break through the mundane to an identification with the myth and ritual they believed. "...through the power of dance and ritual, the dancer performing the movements <u>becomes</u> those things depicted."[102] Drs. Handy and Pukui described from their research that "the old Hawaiian 'did not indulge in art for art's sake.' Whatever artistry was revealed in a performance was only a means toward achieving the overall outcome of the ritual: maximizing the presence of the sacred, divine power, the *mana*."[103]

[Building the hut at the heiau]

Work

[101] Kanahele, <u>Ku Kanaka   Stand Tall</u>, p. 128.
[102] Ibid., p. 131.
[103] Ibid.

The activity of work afforded an encounter with God. "Work in old Hawaii had its solemn and sacred side. Every finished piece of work had to be consecrated, and part of the consecration was the sacred feast at which the *akua*, the god who helped in that work, was supposed to be present and to share the feast with the workers who had completed the canoe or the house or whatever was being dedicated."[104] When we finish a project, tax season, the work of a day, do we find God in all and celebrate the God-touched endeavor?

An historian of ancient Hawaii, David Malo put it succinctly: "The building of a canoe was an affair of religion."[105] Malo identifies some of the gods worshiped by those who went up into the mountains to hew out canoes and timber:

"*Ku-pulupulu* (referring to anything cotton-like, from fibers that cover the fern)

Ku-ala-na-wao (the word <u>*Ku*</u> primarily means to stand; also the god, *Ku*; there stands the wilderness)

Ku-maku-halii (*Ku* personified, as the one who clothes the island)

Ku-pepeiao-loa

Ku-pepeiao-poko

Ku-ka-ieie

Ku-palala-ke

Ku-ka-ohia-laka (<u>*ohia*</u> from the tree of this name; said to have a human voice and had an audible grown when cut) also *Lea* (a female deity worshiped by both men and women canoe makers)."[106]

"A canoe maker prays to the goddess Lea before he fells a tree...a nursing mother prays for enough milk to *Nu'akea*, goddess of

---

104. Handy, <u>Ancient Hawaiian Civilization</u>, p. 61.

105. Ibid., p. 112.

106. Fornander, <u>Hawaiian Antiquities</u>, p. 82.

lactation...a fisherman acknowledges his family animal *'aumakua*, the shark, before casting his net...a hula dancer gathering ferns in the forest asks permission of the goddess, *Laka*...healing and medicine were also based on spirituality."[107]

"*'Aumakuas* were (ancestral) guardian spirits. For every kind of work and for everything one did, there were certain *'aumakuas*. At every feast the *'aumakuas* were supposed to be present. Some of whatever food there was—fish or pig or chicken or taro—was presented on the *kuahu*, a sort of little altar set up...for the *'aumakuas*."[108]

Places

Places became instrumental vehicles for contacting God. In ancient Hawaii a countless number of gods presided over one place or another. Gods presided over regions, heavens, the earth, mountains, ocean, directions, winds and storms, precipices, stones, a house, fireplace, fresh water, a doorway, doorstep, etc.[109]

"Many places were *kapu* (restricted for their sacredness) such as a spot in a forest, a promontory, a rocky seashore or a mountain associated with a mythical event or an *akua* (god)."[110]

"Of all the sacred places, none evoked the kind of awe as did planet earth and the cosmos beyond...for many today awe is reserved for our scientific and technological abilities."[111] And Kanahele developed the contrast between the old Hawaiian ways of

---

[107.] Harden, <u>Voices of Wisdom</u>, p. 41.
[108.] Handy, <u>Ancient Hawaiian Civilization</u>, p. 61.
[109.] Malo, <u>Hawaiian Antiquities (Moolelo Hawaii)</u>, p. 83.
[110.] Kanahele, <u>Ku Kanaka Stand Tall</u>, p. 41.
[111.] Ibid., p. 42.

approaching life and contemporary ways: "...whereas we tend to distance ourselves from the world of the sacred as being something 'eerie' and 'uncanny' and therefore irrelevant and impractical, the traditional Hawaiian embraced his *kapu* world, and in doing so, was able to make it much more meaningful and beneficial to his life. We moderns, it seems, are too uneasy, too uncomfortable with the sacred."[112] Perhaps many of us no longer find God very often within the places of our lives because we do not look there with eyes of faith, expecting to find God.

Hidden Pathways

Dying provided a meeting ground with the gods. Part of a wailing call to the dead reveals the lens of faith, seeing the pathway referenced to the god, Kane:

> "...*e Pa'ula e, ua hala aku la ku'u hoa*
> *i ke ala polikua a Kane.*
>
> *O Pa'ula*, my companion has gone on the hidden
> pathway of *Kane*."[113]

---

112. Ibid., p. 44.
113. Handy and Pukui, <u>Polynesian Family System</u>, p. 154.

Images

Physical objects provided a focus for the ancestral deities (*'aumakua*) and for the major gods (*akua*).[114] These took many forms, such as animals, persons or a carved image. As well as keeping images in the temple (*heiau*), other images would be kept in the home for use whenever someone desired.[115] "When form and god come together, the symbolic embodiment of divine power is achieved... for the Hawaiian believer, all the religious symbols point to the things that are sacred, and at the same time participate in what they symbolize."[116]

Since all the gods "reside in the 'heavens' and no human being ever discerned their nature,"[117] idols provided a means of communication with unseen deities whose dimensions remained unknown to mortals. Performing rites before an image imparted power (*mana*) to the idol and to those participating in the rites.

---

[114] Some would also say the locus for the gods, even equating the idol with the god. See Malo, Hawaiian Antiquities (Moolelo Hawaii), p.85.

[115] Cox and Davenport, Hawaiian Sculpture, p. 96.

[116] Kanahele, Ku Kanaka   (Stand Tall), p. 45.

[117] Malo, Hawaiian Antiquities (Moolelo Hawaii), p. 85

While the features of many images reveal anthropomorphic qualities, the ancient Hawaiian found more in these images than mere humanity with superhuman power.[118] They found contact with the divine through these mostly wooden and stone images.[119] Do we today find God through images which point to a reality beyond the surface, and yet do so via shape, color, texture, movement, etc.?

These instances and many others exemplify where many Hawaiians of old were finding God. Assessments of whether the ancient Hawaiians equated the gods with their idols differ. For example, William Dewitt Alexander and David Malo differed in their understandings of ancient Hawaiians in this area. Some think the Hawaiians of old believed in idolatrous superstition.[120] Regardless, we could find God all over like the ancient Hawaiians. To the current high priestess (*kahuna nui*) and to this author, clearly no thing itself is God–nor any person, nor any place.

These reveal God. We can get in touch with God by using the senses, contemplating the many gifts God gives us, as St. Ignatius Loyola recommends in his Spiritual Exercises,[121] understanding and appreciating them with faith. While finding God in these images of ancient Hawaii may at times resemble totemism, no idea of the gods descending from an animal prevailed.[122] "The

---

[118.] Cox and Davenport, Hawaiian Sculpture, p. 16.

[119.] The larger temple images probably were more vulnerable to destruction since these could not be removed easily and hidden from the 1820's Christian efforts to destroy these icons. 35 larger images and 65 smaller, portable religious images still exist today. See Cox and Davenport, Hawaiian Sculpture, p. 23.

[120.] Malo, Hawaiian Antiquities (Moolelo Hawaii), p. 81 ff.

[121.] David L. Fleming, S.J., The Spiritual Exercises of St. Ignatius: A Literal Translation and A Contemporary Reading. St. Louis: The Institute of Jesuit Sources, 1978, p. 138 ff. Also see Rev. William A.M. Peters, S.J., The Spiritual Exercises of St. Ignatius: Exposition and Interpretations. Jersey City: The Program to Adapt The Spiritual Exercises, 1968, p. 153 ff.

word idol is commonly used, but we must remember that the Hawaiians probably did not worship their idols any more than Catholics worship statues of the Virgin Mary. These images were shrines which the gods could be induced to enter on occasions, to be consulted or asked for help...that the idols themselves were not gods is evidenced by the common custom of making a new image for every ceremony of importance, even though the old one might be kept as still retaining some of the sacredness it had previously possessed."[123]   Dr. Pukui corroborates this perspective when she states: "sometimes people have these stones which help them, but when a stone becomes troublesome, they take it out to sea, drop it, and then turn right around and never look back."[124]   When one symbol for finding God seemed unhelpful, they looked for another.

Ignatius Loyola pointed the seeker to recognize the Giver behind the gift.[125] Schooled in the spirit and teaching in the Bible, Ignatius alerted us to find God and not simply settle for the person, place or thing itself which may catch the eye, the mind, the heart. "But either fire or wind or the swift air or the circuit of stars or the mighty water or the luminaries of heaven, the governors of the world, they considered gods. Now if out of joy in their beauty they thought them gods, let them know how far more excellent is the Lord than these; for the original source of beauty fashioned them."[126] St. Paul cautioned that we be true to God, worshiping the Creator and not merely the creature. He also states forcefully that ever since the creation of the world, God's "invisible attributes of eternal power

---

[122.] Cox and Davenport, Hawaiian Sculpture, p. 14.
[123.] Handy, Ancient Hawaiian Civilization, p. 229.
[124.] Kanahele, Ku Kanaka Stand Tall, p. 46.
[125.] St. Ignatius Loyola, The Spiritual Exercises, no. 235. Also see no. 23.
[126.] Wisdom 13: 2-3.

and divinity have been able to be understood and perceived in what he has made."[127]

Ignatius, as well as *kahuna nui* Momi Mo'okini Lum, invite an openness to finding God everywhere, all around us today. What may at a quick glance appear as animism, instead alerts the seeker to find the one God in all the many ways where God reveals. In ancient Hawaii, "*kino lau* refers to the many forms or bodies both the major gods (*akuas*) and the personalized ancestral gods (*'aumakuas*) could take. These deities could assume the forms of animal, plant or mineral, changing back and forth at will."[128] Today Momi Mo'okini Lum encourages all to pay close attention, with all the faculties available to us, to whatever ways the one God continues to reach out to us. We may find to our surprise and delight that the God who genuinely loves us engages us through the ordinary persons, places and things of our contemporary lives. The engaging continues if only we remain open to it with faith.[129]

E hahai ano no ke kolekole i
kahi nui a ka wahie, a e haha ana no ke 'ino i kahi nui o Ka
pa'akai.

Underdone meat follows along even where wood is plentiful, and decomposition follows along even where much salt is found.

[Even where good is found, evil creeps in].[130]

[127.] Romans 1:16-25.

[128.] Pukui, Haertig and Lee, Nana I Ke Kumu (Look To The Source), Vol 1, p. 125.

[129.] Personal interview with Zita Leimomi Mo'okini Lum 19 November 2003.

[130.] Pukui, 'Olelo: Proverbs, p. 34, no.271.

Part of the struggle of our human journey involves deciphering when God is communicating with us and how this differs from evil creeping in under the guise of good. We need to discern the movements of God as we and the Hawaiians of old do not always "agree on the interpretation of these signs."[131]

St. Ignatius Loyola offered rules of thumb to distinguish movements of God from those not of God. Among them, for a person committed to a relationship with God and living a godly life, those experiences which foster deeper inner peace and consolation give evidence of being from God. Whereas for someone prone to cutting corners and living a careless, sinful life—one which would never be described as godly—the presence of God is discerned via the inner turmoil and dissatisfaction with continuing along careless ways which are not of God.[132]

The Hawaiians of old recognized as well the need to clarify whether something was from God or bogus. Drs. Pukui, Haertig and Lee put it this way: "How much a revelation comes from the spirit or from personal fears or wishes is difficult to distinguish...the *ho ike* (wise understanding of revelation), the immediate, awesome, emotion-charged flash of knowledge, carried mystic overtones."[133] The wisdom (*ike*) to know what comes from God remains itself a gift from God. We need to pray for this wisdom to discern the inner movements from God. Often after prayer about a matter, we need to set it aside and trust that in God's time (not ours), God will bring clarity to the discernment if we need it. God does not operate to our drum beat. We do not demand and get our every whim or want.

[131.] Fornander, Hawaiian Antiquities, p. 134.

[132.] St. Ignatius Loyola, The Spiritual Exercises, no. 314-315 of the Rules for the Discernment of Spirits.

[133.] Pukui, Haertig, and Lee, Nana I Ke Kumu (Look to the Source), Vol. 1, p. 44.

We need language to communicate with God and with each other about finding God. Sometimes this language embodies words; sometimes forms other than words work better. In describing how symbols are the language of the sacred, George Kanahele writes: "Unless one understands and speaks the language of the sacred, the world it tries to report remains forever in the eerie distance. Thus, for Hawaiians of old, religious or sacred symbolism served a far more vital function than it does for the secularized people of today."[134] We need ways not only to understand and to be understood as we express our relationship with God and all else in this context, but also to cultivate these sacred relationships. Mary Kawena Pukui said it this way: "Without *pule*, without prayer, I think my people would be lost."[135] The prayer language of myth and ritual "wrapped in metaphors, poetic images, similes, allegories, word play, *kaona* (hidden meaning)...convey mystical experience...mythology tells about the world of the sacred, the supernatural, about the gods and their deeds. To Hawaiians of old then, mythology was the most important of their creations–and the most real...today myth is often understood as 'unreal,' 'fantasy,' 'make-believe,' meaning nothing to the real, concrete, practical empirical world we know."[136]

Both *kahuna nui*, Momi Mo'okini Lum, and this author recognize and encourage the development of both a verbal and non-verbal language which defies the power of ordinary speech and action, and conveys and cultivates contact with God. Finding God provides one dimension; developing a relationship with God moves the finding to another, deeper level. With an ongoing, deepening relationship with God, we discover a new lens. This new lens of

[134.] Kanahele, <u>Ku Kanaka Stand Tall</u>, p. 44.
[135.] Ibid., p. 128.
[136.] Ibid., p. 48 ff. Also see Joseph Campbell, <u>The Hero With A Thousand Faces</u>.

faith is a gift. While we cannot obtain the gift on our own effort alone, often we have received even the smallest lens (like the mustard seed in the gospel) but we do not use it. Use it or lose it.

When asked by his companions to put in writing his experience of the month-long encounter alone with God (retreat), Ignatius Loyola's writing was called the <u>Spiritual Exercises</u>. As regular physical exercise tones the body, spiritual *exercises* tone the spirit, develop a vital spiritual life. Exercising regular communication with God alone (private prayer) and with other people of faith (common prayer, liturgy) both enables us to express our spiritual vision and to clarify and to refine it, as our relationship with God and people of God nuances and deepens.

Part Three: Cultivating Gratitude

"Mai nana i ka 'ulu o waho
'a'ohe ia nau; e nana no i ka
'ulu i ke alo, nau ia.

Never mind looking for the breadfruit way out, that is not for you; look at the breadfruit in front of you, that is yours.

[Be satisfied with what you have]."[137]

How often we confuse need and greed. Is there ever enough? Do we appreciate all that we have and find ways to express our gratitude toward those responsible for all we have?

[137.] Pukui, *'Olelo: Proverbs*, p. 226, no. 2080.

In the USA cultural climate which breeds and feeds on a mentality of consumerism, readily messages seep into us which cultivate a desire for more, different, newer, older, easier, etc. The more "stuff," the more we need to integrate and, hopefully with a grateful heart. Unfortunately, the cluttering of our lives tends to confuse needing and wanting. Really, do we need half of what we want? Surreptitiously a surly attitude creeps into us which, if we are not careful, sours our spirit. Our hearts become callused, preoccupied with obtaining the next possession to titillate our fancy. Does this way of living help us cultivate an attitude of gratitude? Actually, it undermines our cultivating gratitude. By contrast, usually after taking what the Hawaiian of old needed from the forest, "...you pray your thanks before you leave."[138] To grab and go, without care for appreciating what we receive, accentuates the "gimme" approach so prevalent in our USA culture. This selfish attitude worsens sometimes when a "you-owe-me" sense accompanies the "grab-and-go" *modus operandi* because of choosing inadequate time to savor with a grateful heart.

Within the context of ancient Hawaii, most people believed that the *'aumakuas* (ancestral gods) guided their family members away from dangerous attitudes and situations and toward more life-giving ways. Similar to beliefs around guardian angels in the Roman Catholic Church, *'aumakuas* would personally protect and encourage living with a spirit of gratitude for the gifts God lavishes upon us.[139] The gospel of John puts it this way: "...grace upon grace."[140] God

---

[138.] Kahu 'Iokepaokalani (Fr. Joseph L. Priestly, S.M.), Hawaiian Spirituality. Honolulu: Marianist Hall, 2000, p. 12.

[139.] Personal interview with Zita Leimomi Mo'okini Lum 12 November 2003.

[140.] John: 1: 16

provides one gift on top of another, each day. Can we work at and play with appreciating the gift upon gift which God bestows upon us? We can. What prevents us from doing so?

Our pace of living as well as greed blurs our vision. We accustom ourselves with accelerating our pace to keep up with or to get ahead of those around us. The norm for choice: others. Paying insufficient attention to our own inner rhythms distorts us. Acting on the gospel incorporated in *our* lives will establish a stable foundation which can weather stormy times and yield life which satisfies and lasts.[141] Living a full life says much more about life's quality than its quantity. If we were to choose regular reflection to punctuate our day, we would find cultural vectors fighting such a choice. Quieting down in the midst of noise within and without would challenge the faint of heart. For we imbibe prevailing cultural messages about the contemporary value of multi-tasking and praise for getting the "jump" on the slowness of others because "snooze you lose" and "the early bird catches the worm." Choosing periodic quiet moments to become more alert to the God-given gifts within us and around us takes quiet reflection. Otherwise we can easily miss them "on the fly."

Another blinder which prevents seeing gifts of God: we allow the culture to predispose us to be on the lookout for the <u>next</u> gift even before we appropriate the one before us. Spoiled as brats, we lose a sense of gratitude for what we have before us and instead go for the next gift we might get if we pushed. A story about a child from an impoverished situation illustrates the point. An older retired lady felt sorry for this little kid, especially during Christmas time.

[141.] Matthew: 7: 24

She had noticed him before, prayed for him and said hello; but this time she invited him to her house for something to eat. She prepared a lavish meal–the kind a kid would love: thick and juicy burgers and fries and a milk shake, etc. When she presented him with a piece of homemade apple pie, still warm from the oven and the luscious aromas wafting around, she placed the huge wedge of pie before him with a poignant gesture, communicating the sense of "Ta-dah...isn't this the *piece de resistance!*" The young boy looked up at her with a quizzical look and exclaimed: what, lady, no cheese? We can be the same way with God sometimes. Preoccupied with obtaining the next pleasureful gift, we fail to see and to savor the good gifts given us even at that very moment and fail to say thank you to God...and to those people instrumental in God's ways of caring for us.

Have we ever found ourselves preoccupied with opening the next Christmas present without adequately appreciating the thought and care of the giver that went into the gift we just opened–not to mention appreciating the gift itself? Often while working with university students over the last thirty years, we witnessed how many rationalize flitting from one experience to the next, attempting to justify their choices by saying this is all part of the "college experience." Efforts to alert students to recognize and to appreciate and to appropriate the gifts right before them fly in the face of prevailing collegial tendencies to jump quickly, sometimes recklessly, from one experience to another without adequate reflection, gratitude and integration.

Mindful of the gospel story of Jesus healing ten lepers with only one of the ten returning to give thanks,[142] we can find solace in

---

[142.] Luke 17: 11-19.

recognizing that God's gratuity does not depend upon our gratitude. God gives freely, without strings attached. Of course, this provides no excuse for persisting with our ingratitude, barreling on ahead in search of more goodies without appreciating the gift given, and especially the Giver.

Binging can become another cultural blinder in the USA today. Disguised as living life in the "fast lane" and living with "gusto," binging at work as well as at play can stymie the nudging of God toward developing a grateful heart. "Work hard, play hard" parades across our American consciousness (and subconsciousness) in overt and subliminal ways. These kinds of messages inculcate an approach to life which leaves little room for savoring, for relishing the gift, let alone the Giver. Often the culture lures us into putting our heads down and charging forward, with inadequate time in the present moment. No time to stroll. Forget snail mail. We need to find ways to balance our American values of pragmatism and efficiency with recovery of *virtus stat in medio* (virtue stands in the middle)[143] and the Greek golden mean. Ever notice how much easier it is for us to work all this out in theory and in words than in life? The culture is sick and the frame of reference is contagious.

Fear of intimacy blinds many of us from seeing and receiving more fully all the gifts God lavishes upon us. It remains easier to skim the surface than to delve deeply, especially in relationships with God, self and others.

However, what a quantitative and qualitative shift in happiness occurs when we brave our fear of being too close for

---

[143.] St. Thomas Acquinas, <u>Summa Theologica</u>, Question 64, Article 1.

comfort. For happiness is a byproduct. We do not achieve it by charging after happiness directly. Rather, happiness and pervasive sense of well-being, *joi de vive*, arrive when we establish right relationships, especially with God. If this relationship is sound, our ways of relating to self and others will evolve along similar lines, in the image of our God-relationship.

As people of faith, followers of Jesus believe God gives his very self in Jesus–and gives abundantly. How often in a year do we recall the words of Jesus: "I have come that they may have life and have it abundantly"?[144] And in another section of the gospel, Jesus says: "...that my joy may be yours and your joy may be complete."[145] Yet even for people of faith, we too fall prey to taking the path of least resistance, finding intimacy (especially with God) easier to talk about and to write about than to actually live.

Common sense seems less than common these days. After all, who would not characterize themselves as grateful people? In addressing the believers in Rome, St. Paul said:
"...for although they knew God, they did not accord him glory as God, or give him thanks."[146] *Kahuna nui* Momi Mo'okini Lum often describes how the Hawaiians of old always started their prayer thanking the gods for all they had BEFORE ever asking for what they thought they needed.[147] Do we?   Many of us have forgotten how to say thank you. In describing the Makahiki festival of ancient Hawaii, Samuel Manaiakalani Kamakau stated: "They gave thanks

---

[144.] John 10: 10.

[145.] John 15: 11.

[146.] Romans 1: 21.

[147.]   Personal interview with Zita Lemomi Mo'okini Lum 26 November 2003.

to the god (Lono) for his care, and for his help; from him came life, blessings, peace and victory." By contrast, often we become blase about our gifts until a threat to their presence occurs through an accident or illness or perhaps the body or mind no longer function as they once did when younger.

The *common* sense about the gifts of our lives: these are merely impersonal "givens," facts. We need to take initiative. Choose to move away from taking the efforts of a teacher or of a parent for granted. Look twice at our children or at our brothers and sisters, at our appliances in the house, at the gift of a stomach which functions well. We can change our minds and hearts after reassessing whether our gifts embody "pure luck of the draw" or mysterious gifts.

To rely on a common spiritual sense in our contemporary American culture seems fallacious. We need to work at clarifying a truer picture and play with possibilities about who and what is really good about our lives. Identify the persons, places and things, the experiences which mean something to us. At our time and place our awareness of these good gifts can elude us.

Part of moving away from taking these goods for granted involves naming them for ourselves and for those we consider closer to us. "Talking story," communicating with someone about our inner life (what matters to us and why and how), remains a vital part of Hawaiian culture to this day.[148] Often when we hear ourselves speak about aspects of our inner life, we discover in some new and deeper ways what gifts they are. Often when those we love and trust respond to our "talking story," they open new horizons for

---

[148.] Ibid. 19 December 2003.

us. We lowered our guard enough, imagining that of all people, these love and trust us enough to tell the truth and not simply "yes" us to death. Their honest, transparent response affords us a view of the goods of our lives from fresh perspectives.

Another aspect of cultivating gratitude for the good gifts of our lives, the most important aspect, involves seeing and sensing the connection between the gifts and God. The psalmist in the Bible alerts those willing to learn: "The heavens proclaim the glory of God, and the firmament proclaims his handiwork."[149] Yet not everyone makes this connection. Some look at an exceptional sunset or mountain or architecture of a city and, if they notice and acknowledge anything, they will simply say something like: that is beautiful.

We have to see with eyes of faith to recognize that God gives this gift. To the person of faith, all the world did not just happen and the skylines and cityscapes and technologies give eloquent testimony to God as well as humanity. God loved us first, the Bible reminds

---

[149.] Psalm 19.

us,[150] and God provides us with what we need to live here and forever. At our best, the spirit animating all the endeavors of humanity reveals that the touch of God continues to create freely and to salvage us in Jesus when we get distorted. What a God-given, privileged point of view: to be able to recognize the connection between God and our gifts. God does not reserve this point of view to the privileged few, but in Jesus opens this way of seeing to all people.[151] But with privileges come responsibilities.

A potent way of responding to recognizing the divine dimension of the gifts would be to ritually renew the commitment to God with a grateful heart and to the faith community gathered for the ritual.[152] Thanking those who had a hand in providing the good gifts becomes a conduit for relationships with God, others and self. A power comes from the ritual exercise of thanking the One responsible for everything being God-touched. While discussing the role of myth and ritual in Hawaiian society of old, George Hu'ue Sanford Kanahele described a twofold purpose of ritual: "to replenish one's spiritual power or *mana*, and to maximize one's capacity to experience and to know the ultimate meaning and significance of life."[153]

Regularly we all lose perspective, which substantiates the need to come together for religious myth and ritual. God's Word enlightens our perspective so that we can see and sense again–the whole picture and the parts of the picture which lost focus. Common prayer around the Bible readings and the table of the Lord help us

---

[150.] 1 John 4: 19.
[151.] Preface for Epiphany, The Sacramentary, p. 385.
[152.] Kanahele, Ku Kanaka Stand Tall, p. 108.
[153.] Ibid., p. 104.

remember what we so easily forget and help us give thanks for what we so easily take for granted. Breaking open the meanings of God's point of view in the proclaimed scripture often can provide a real sense of God's presence. The gathered community of believers cultivates in another way that God is with us. Certainly the Eucharist cultivates gratitude for the presence of the Lord being real and with us. For example, within the introductory dialogue of every Preface at Mass, the presider says: "Let us give thanks to the Lord our God." And the entire assembly responds: "It is right to give him thanks and praise."[154] This same dynamic occurred in the Hawaiian temple rituals of old: "...the deeds of the gods were recounted in the *mo'olelo* (story, history, legend). Or, in other words, ritual is the re-enactment of supernatural actions or events applied to human endeavors."[155]

Liturgy, common worship in the Christian tradition, cultivates ways of being in the world which often challenge the current mentalities and behaviors in the American scene. For example, is the only reason for choosing to worship with others because I need it? So we choose to participate in common worship only when we as individuals need it? Is even liturgy only self-serving? Surely the almighty God does not need liturgy, as the American bishops reminded us in 1978;[156] but depriving the assembly of believers of our faithful presence (not to mention our spouse, family and friends, colleagues at work, etc.) affects the fabric of community, as well as the individual. Liturgical words and

---

154. The Sacramentary. New York: Catholic Book Publishing Company, 1985, p. 548.

155. Kanahele, Ku Kanaka Stand Tall, p. 103

156. Bishops Committee on the Liturgy, " Environment and the Art in Catholic Worship" No. 4 in The Liturgy Documents: A Parish Resource, Vol. 1. Chicago Liturgy Training Publication, 1991, p.319.

gestures can challenge us to think "outside the box" and to be less concerned with grabbing the next gift rather than noticing and appreciating the gifts right before our eyes.

In liturgy we can imagine what life would be like if we try on for size another way of thinking and acting which would look different from the way we operate currently. We can play with new possibilities for taking gospel ways of living to heart. Then, since we learn on other levels by doing, we can go out and practice at work and at home. We need to incorporate the lens of faith or we will persist in having eyes but not seeing.[157]

We can perceive more by slowing down on a regular basis, by focusing on the gifts before us, by challenging prevailing cultural frames of reference. We can venture forth into taking the next best step toward cultivating a spirit of gratitude in a cultural context in which negativity abounds. Seeing reality with little or no hope, cynicism exists as a common cultural ethos. This embodies anything but a Christian response to life experience. For those who love God, not only **can** God salvage good from every situation (even tragic injury and death), but God **will**, as St. Paul needed to remind the church in Rome during the first generations after Jesus.[158]

"Ihea no ka lima a 'au mai?

Where are the arms with which to swim?

[Don't complain, use your limbs to do what you need to do.]"[159]

---

157. Ezekiel 12 : 2 .
158. Romans 8: 28.

We can fritter away so much energy and opportunity by complaining. The wisdom of ancient Hawaii acknowledged the reality of our fractured human situation as well. Even in this tropical paradise, people complain about everything from weather to health to politics, etc., just like everywhere else in the world. Far from perfect, the human condition provides ample opportunity for griping. If ever we get on a roll in the direction of selectively perceiving what is wrong in the world (our individual world, our household, our church, our larger society, etc.), we will find ample evidence of imperfection...and likely choke off our awareness of gratitude for wonderful gifts within us and around us. When our predominant spirit becomes sour and cynical and the pattern becomes complaining more than thanking, *attentione*! Something is wrong, radically wrong in our response to God's lavishing us with gifts. Instead, as the Hawaiian proverb suggests, we need to use our God-given abilities to recognize, to appreciate, to enjoy our gifts and to share them with so many under our roof and in our world who need them. Let us make use of what we have as gifts from God, cultivating a grateful heart.

[159.] Pukui, *'Olelo: Proverbs*, p. 126, no. 1155.

Part Four: Restoring Sacrifice

"Ka ha'awi a ka mea hale, koe
koena 'ole ma ku'ono

Giving as a house owner does,
with nothing left in the corners.

[Said of a very generous person who gives freely of all he has.]"[160]

Our generation of believers brings something valuable to the table. We appropriated significant aspects of the Christian tradition and enculturated them for our time and American place in ways which promote the faith. We recovered aspects of the tradition which had been lost or at least de-emphasized. For example, due to such an emphasis on Jesus being God, many lost a visceral sense that Jesus was really a human being, like us in all things but sin.[161] Yet,

---

160. Pukui, *'Olelo*: Proverbs, p. 140, no. 1286.

like the swing of the proverbial pendulum, our generation of Christians needs to face aspects of our tradition which wane. A half century or more ago, as we Americans were rebuilding our own country and others' from the devastation of a major world war, we knew sacrifice in our bones. As Catholics, we prayed the Holy Sacrifice of the Mass. Sacrifice was not only a more regular part of our vocabulary, but also of our thinking, believing and choosing.

Today presents another matter. For example, even though Catholics pray the word sacrifice (or the equivalent) eight times in Eucharistic Prayer II alone[162] (not to mention the number of times it occurs frequently in the Bible readings and other prayers at every Mass), do we develop a cultural glaze over the eyes and the heart and not see and sense the sacrificial connection with Jesus in the circumstances of our lives? Our American culture seems hell-bent on convenience, comfort and pleasure almost at all costs. "Kubla Kahn," the poem of the eighteenth century poet Samuel Taylor Coleridge seems to describe the American fantasy: "In Xanadu did Kubla Kahn a stately pleasure dome decree..." The pleasure principle is alive and well in our country at this time. Many of us think and talk about living for the weekend or for the next break, as if there is no living at work. So for most of the week (40-70 hours+ of work), we gut it out. A common mentality these days: if we can just get past this project or difficulty or deadline of some kind which seems costly, THEN we can live. What is the living for? Pleasure? Ease? What does it mean to l-i-v-e?

If we simply go with the cultural flow, easy-come/easy-go predominates our consciousness. Even more, what eludes our

---

161. The Sacramentary. New York: Catholic Book Publishing Company, 1985, p. 557.

162. The Sacramentary, p. 548 ff.

awareness? For Instance, what in our culture inclines us toward sacrifice? In life as we have experienced it the last decades in the USA, the notion of sacrifice has receded into the background and living as comfortably as possible has replaced it. We hear and speak, "What is in it for me?" This militates against the genuine spirit of Christ and the spirit of *Aloha*. As *kahuna nui* Momi Mo'okini Lum addressed God for the opening session of the State House of Representatives in 1998, she prayed: "...Heavenly Father, your people of Hawaii live in troubled times, the very essence of *Aloha* is being challenged..."[163]

Many of us develop stingy ways of operating and thinking, partly because we let ourselves get pulled in so many directions and we hanker for the oasis around the corner. Real living seems always one small (or large) problem away. Rather than embracing with passion whatever sits on our plate at the moment, often the draw of the greater comfort tends to syphon the power and energy of our heart's desires.

"Luxuries and comforts do not teach some things," *kahuna nui* Mo'okini Lum has stated in confronting the current cultural resistance to sacrifice.[164] And while she works at preserving the best of the past of Hawaiian ways and tries to communicate this especially to the children, she labors at finding better ways to connect with the children and to challenge whatever short- sighted selfishness she encounters. These children come from the real comfort-oriented world of today and they reflect what they learn from those around them. Often self-sacrifice is not high on the list at home. It needs to be and this will require recovery.

[163.] Leimomi Mo'okini Lum, "*Pule* (Prayer) for the Opening Session, House of Represent-atives, State of Hawaii, 21 January 1998," p. 3.

[164.] Personal interview with Zita Leimomi Mo'okini Lum 8 September 2003.

Why? What is so valuable about sacrifice? As the meaning of the opening proverb conveyed, when we embody generosity, we give freely of all we have. Our Christian scriptures propose the same message: give freely from what we have received so freely.[165] We should not give away what we have carelessly or compulsively, but freely. To do so requires enormous self-sacrifice.

The flower *lei* provides a potent symbol of self-sacrifice. We must obtain the flowers, soak them in water, string them and then present the fruit of our labor to someone we care about. The Hawaiians of old presented the first and the finest and the biggest fruit, taro, mats, etc. to god (Lono) during their Makahiki festival.[166] Sacrificing their very best and giving it to God constituted regular ancient Hawaiian ritual practice–and not only once a year. "The common daily worship would seem to have consisted in offering a bit of food (*hanai 'ai*) at the time of eating."[167] Sacrificing some of one's own food to the ancestral gods (*'aumakuas*) and to the major gods (*'akuas*) ritually thanked them for the nourishment and for being with them. "The idea behind the offering to the *'aumakuas* may be compared to the idea behind the Christian celebration of the Lord's Supper or the sacrament of communion. At this sacrament the Lord is supposed to be present in the food shared by the people."[168] We need ritual ways of keeping God at the center of daily life. Do we Hawaiians and mainlanders of today practice expressing and cultivating for ourselves as well as others that God is first and foremost in our minds, in our lives? Many of us today find it

---

[165.] Matthew 10:8.

[166.] Personal interview with Zita Leimomi Mo'okini Lum 25 August 2003.

[167.] Drs. Handy and Pukui, Polynesian Family System, p. 96.

[168.] E.S. Craighill Handy et al., Ancient Hawaiian Civilization. Rutland, VT: Charles E. Tuttle Company Publishers, 1965, p. 61.

burdensome, too much trouble, to sacrifice precious little time in order to pause a moment, to thank God for the meal before us. Even if a formulary prayer such as "Bless us, O Lord, and these your gifts..." seems antiquated and an inadequate contemporary way to express such gratitude, do we find other ways (even silence for a moment) to sacrifice for God and make the meal a sacred activity?

Those who visit the Mo'okini temple (*heiau*) in Kohala on the Big Island frequently bring flowers to offer to God, as a symbol of offering themselves to God. The sacrifice of time and energy and expense involved in obtaining the flowers and reverently placing them upon the altar as an offering to God conveys and cultivates the relationship with God. Leimaker and author, Marie McDonald, in Voices of Wisdom stated in response to people who ask how to make a flower *lei* last: "It really bothers me because this is not the reason for the *lei*–that it should last forever. What should last is the thought, the reason for giving that *lei*, the thought that went into it. Words can be beautiful, but sometimes 'I love you' is not enough. If you say it with something as beautiful as a *lei*, you know there is a lot of power in that."[169] In cherishing the perishable (precious and fragile flowers) and most of all the imperishable (the spirit behind the gift and especially the giver), the sacrificing seems valuable, worthwhile.

While explicating the beauty of spring and what we can learn to incorporate in our lives from the vernal lessons, Parker Palmer describes spring as "a great give-away of blooming– beyond all necessity and reason...for no reason than the sheer joy of it...if you receive a gift, you keep it alive not by clinging to it, but by passing it along."[170]

---

[169]. M.J. Harden, ed., Voices of Wisdom, p. 185.
[170]. Parker Palmer, Let Your Life Speak. San Francisco: Josey-Bass,

In fact, the Bible tells us how much better it is to give than receive,[171] and Jesus clearly modeled in word and action that he (and his followers) came to serve rather than to be served.[172] When teaching about the myth of Santa Claus, many students laugh at first hearing that I continue to believe in Santa. While not putting out milk and cookies since early childhood, in my adult years I came to value the sacrifice required to give others without expecting anything in return. Many of us adult Americans do not believe in this kind of giving and do not practice it. Is it any wonder that we grow in self-gratification rather than self-sacrifice?

After thirty years of teaching and living in residence halls with students, I have learned volumes from my students. Among the lessons, many students are hungry especially later in the evening and they genuinely appreciate home-cooking, which rarely appears when students live on campus. Since I know contemporary students well and also since I like to cook, regularly I will stroll through the residence halls and offer the students some of the food. For example, when I see a couple students, I will say hello and then ask: are you hungry? Would you like some pasta? Over the years I have discovered multiple filters which initially prevent students from readily receiving the food. A ritual barrage of their questions and my answers ensues as the academic year begins:

- Question: what is this? Answer: it's pasta.

- Question: what does it cost? Answer: nothing.

2000, p. 105.
    [171.] Acts 20:35.
    [172.] Matthew 20:28, Mark 10:45.

[Students learn quickly that almost everything is pro-rated and the University passes along as many costs as possible.]

- Question: what kind of a program is this? Answer: it's not a program, I like to cook and I thought those of you who are hungry might like some.

- Question: what if I'm not a Catholic? Answer: I think it will still go down!

- Question: what if I don't believe in Confession? Answer: okay, but I didn't even bring up the topic...I only brought pasta–would you like some?

Geez...(and I start to walk away and say) you don't h-a-v-e t-o eat some to graduate. I just thought you would like some home-made food.

In the end, they will usually take some and be surprised that they find it flavorful, as good or better than Mom's and Dad's.

What does this annual ritual reveal? Students find it hard to believe that someone would give without hooks. There must be some hidden agenda or sneaky pay-off. So much of the world operates this way, sad to say. Even much of our University. Again, Jesus revealed the truth that in reality it is better for us to give than to receive;[173] but many of us experience this rarely, if ever, even within our families and faith communities.

[173.] Acts of the Apostles 20:35.

Two of the ancient Hawaiian proverbs preserved by Mary Kawena Pukui evidence the self-sacrificing spirit alive in Hawaii of old.

*"I hele i kauhale, pa'a pu'olo i
ka lima."*

In going to the houses of others,
carry a package in the hand.

[Take a gift.][174]

"Ko koa uka, ko koa kai.

Those of the upland, those of the shore.

[In olden days relatives and friends exchanged products. The upland dwellers brought *poi*, *taro*, and other foods to the shore to give to kinsmen there. The shore dweller gave fish and other seafood. Visits were never made empty-handed but always with something from one's home to give.][175]

How often do we embody this spirit of self-sacrifice? In our part of the world at this time these practices seem rare. We could choose to bring a gift, sacrificing the time and care and financial cost to think about what others might enjoy and appreciate from what is available to us. We could treat someone to a dessert or to flowers or to a photograph. Among the values of sacrifice, symbolically let others (including God) know that we care about them. The *kahuna nui* (high priestess of the Mo'okini line of the indigenous Hawaiian

---

[174.] Pukui, *'Olelo: Proverbs*, p.126, no. 1157.
[175.] Ibid., p. 196-197, no. 1821.

religion) puts it this way to the children: "Caring is sharing."[176] This sounds simple, but we feel the cost when offering others (sacrificing) some of our favorite Doritos or chocolates, the best piece of meat on the serving platter, some of precious time and energy. The ante escalates significantly when we risk offering some of our very self, our own inner life, to others. What it means to others can validate the value of sacrifice. Truth be told, sometimes others do not appreciate our sacrifice, though God always does. Even if others do not understand and appreciate, we have the inner peace and satisfaction of knowing that our heart was in the right place. And when the other does receive our sacrifice, a sense of significant union occurs–communion.[177] At one with each other, we sense a real presence of love. Mindful of the scriptural verse in the first letter of John, "where there is love there is God,"[178] often we have a palpable awareness of God being with us. Is this experience not analogous to the experience of receiving Jesus at Eucharist?

A similar experience of sharing occurred in ancient Hawaiian rite of passage. As a young boy of four or five he left eating and living with the women and ritually entered the *mua*, the eating and lounging and praying house of the men. The *mua* contained an altar (*kuahu*) at one end of the house with images of the familial ancestral gods (*'aumakuas*). The father of the transitioning young boy would bake a pig and offer the head on the altar. The father offered ritual drink (*'awa*) as well. Part of the ritual prayer accompanying this rite of passage follows:

"*Ala mai, e Lono, i kou haina awa, haina awa noui nou, e Lono*

[176.] Personal interview with Zita Leimomi Mo'okini Lum 8 September 2003.

[177.] Communion derives from the Latin-*cum* meaning with and *unus* meaning one.

[178.] 1 John 4 :16.

he ula mai, e Kea, he pepeio puaa, he pepeio ilio, he pepeio
aina nui–nou, e Lono...

Arise, O *Lono*, and accept the offerings of *'awa* to you–an
important offering, O *Lono*.
Great abundance, O Kea, may there be an abundance of
hog's and dog's ears–an abundance for you to eat, O *Lono*."[179]

When a fundamental rupture in a relationship occurs, it needs
reconciliation. When we reflect on the origin of the word
reconciliation, we savor the significance of coming eyelash to
eyelash with God, self and others again. Who modeled this repair
work better than Jesus, who "died once for all?"[180] A sacrifice raw
and total, the ultimate cost of faithful love, putting his one human
life on the altar of the cross for all humanity. Saving us seemed
valuable to God. Yet often we seem impervious to the depth of
meaning here and somewhat disinterested. Fortunately God cares
enough to save us from ourselves, our own self-built prison walls.

Sacrificial self-giving can mend the fractures of the human
heart and help restore relationships. In Jesus we witness this most
clearly. In ancient Hawaii, only a king could construct a *luakini*
heiau (a special royal temple), of the highest order. The Mo'okini
heiau was constructed as one of these special temples, a *luakini*.

[179.] Handy and Pukui, <u>Polynesian Family System</u>, p. 97.
[180.] Hebrews 10: 10.

Originally only the king and chiefs, the royalty (*'alii*) and the priests (*kahunas*, the highest ranking being the *kahuna nui*) could worship in this luakini. The *kahunas* of this rite outranked others and only in this *luakini* would human sacrifice be offered.[181]

When Momi Mo'okini Lum became high priestess in 1977,[182] she prayed for two years for the *ike* (wisdom) to know how to open this temple for the children–the expressed vision of her uncle and confirmed by her father, the two *kahuna nui* before her. In 1979 she lifted one *kapu* (sacred rule), forever eliminating human sacrifices from occurring in the temple so that children would be welcome. Flowers, especially the *lei*, would now symbolize the self, self-sacrifice, placing ourselves on the altar to God.

During an address at Scholfield Army Base in 1993, someone in the group of military chaplains confronted *kahuna nui* Momi Mo'okini Lum about the incomprehensibility of human sacrifice. The *kahuna nui* paused a moment, turned around and simply gestured toward the crucifix in the room...and spoke about Jesus as the human sacrifice for us all. Not only did Jesus pay the mortal

---

[181] Malo, Hawaiian Antiquities, (Moolelo Hawaii), p.159.

[182] According to genealogical chants, the Mo'okini *luakini* dates back to 480 A.D. Momi is only the seventh female *kahuna* in the Mo'okini line. The other six are buried near the *heiau* in North Kohala on the Big Island.

price of faithful love, but also he freely laid down his life to set us all free. Giving God our best, we would be in right relationship with God, ourselves and each other. Like no other, Jesus could and did make up for what was lacking in us. No longer would selfishness and sin reign. Death would continue as a word in the human story, but in Jesus never again would it be the last word. Rather <u>life</u>, the full fruition of self-sacrificing love.

God reads the heart.[183]   Only God knows whether we give from our surplus or we risk sacrificing what remains cherished to us for the sake of God and others. The gospel story about the poor widow who gave a couple copper coins worth a few cents[184] reveals this central message: God knows. We can fool many people, but not God.   Based on appearances, we humans might think this impoverished widow contributed a mere pittance and the rich man who gave lots more money to be the real hero. In fact, Jesus reverses this understanding because God reads the heart. The truth of the matter: this woman sacrificed from her very substance and the rich man from his surplus. Jesus praises her as the heroine. A follower of Jesus ought to emulate the kind of sacrifice of the poor widow in order to come alive.

Appearances can deceive. God does not assess the way we humans do.[185] God knows if we rest on our laurels, comfortably content to give here and there. Of course, if our contribution helps, however regular and in whatever amount, then it is worth doing. For example, a wise man directed me as a Jesuit novice, during my first years of learning about the interior life of the spirit. One time when in a quandary, I remember seeking his advice. I wondered if I

[183.] Jeremiah 17:10, 1 Chronicles 29:17.
[184.] Mark 12: 42, Luke 21:2.
[185.] 1 Samuel 16: 12.

should bring some flowers to a friend. Responding to his query about the cause of my unease, I described my worry that my bringing of the flowers intended to get her to like me. In his unnerving way he smiled at me and said: would she enjoy the flowers? That was a "no brainer" to answer, but his subsequent comment served me for a lifetime: then always do what you know will help people and clean up your motives along the way. Regularly our human motivation needs purifying, yet we should never deprive others of our good gifts because we need purification. Yet, we should not attempt to play games with God. The truth sets us free, even when it reveals parts of ourselves which we wish were different.

Learning how to give not only what we own and can buy, but also of our very self requires sacrifice. We can invest much of ourselves in giving money, prayer, time, energy, food, expertise to those who need these good gifts. The Hawaiians of old provide eloquent, living examples of such self-sacrificing generosity. Drs. Pukui, Haertig and Lee describe a potent example. The true *kanaka makua* (mentally and emotionally mature) person "has the prized Hawaiian attitude–he must be hospitable...Mrs. Pukui points out that the traditional *kanaka makua* behavior included 'calling out to visitors when you saw them coming '*Heahea! Kahea 'ai!* (Welcome! Come on in. Come in and eat!) This hospitality connoted a warm and generous giving and sharing, whether of food or companionship or concern and comfort, always in a person-to-person way. He has outgrown the infantile grasping to get all one can and keep all one has...' "[186]   While many examples of Hawaiian self-sacrifice permeated the indigenous culture, hospitality (*ho'okipa*) surely left its mark. "Hospitality was the rule; stinginess

---

[186.] Pukui, Haertig and Lee, <u>Nana I Ke Kumu (Look to the Source)</u>, Vol 1, p.118.

was beyond contempt. *'Kahea 'ai...'Ai a ma'ona'* (come in and eat...eat all you want) was the accepted greeting, even to comparative strangers."[187] Giving of one's self as well as of one's things provided a constitutive element of the ancient Hawaiian culture.[188]

> "*'A 'ohe ia e loa'a aku, he ulua*
> *kapapa no ka moana*
>
> He cannot be caught for he is an
> ulua fish of the deep ocean.

[said in admiration of a hero or warrior who will not give up without a struggle.]"[189]

So many of us contemporary Americans seem unwilling to fight for something or someone. Perhaps this is because we have not loved. Only when we genuinely care for something or someone would we take a stand and say this is worth fighting for. Perhaps the response of some in the USA to the 911 terrorism provides an exception to this recent pattern.

What makes something worth a fight, even if the fighting causes pain? Certainly the motivation for braving pain should not evidence pathology, e.g., it hurts so good. Finding pleasure in the pain of the fight remains far from a Christian motivation. If love motivates the sacrifice, only then will it bring life.

> "*Kauwa ke aloha i na lehua o Ka'ana.*

---

[187] Ibid. p. 7.

[188] Personal interview Zita Leimomi Mo'okini Lum10 October 2003.

[189] Pukui, *'Olelo*: Proverbs, p. 18, no. 145.

Love is a slave to the *lehua* blossoms of Ka'ana.

[Ka'ana is a place where travelers used to rest and make a *lei* of the *lehua*. It took many blossoms and much patience to complete a *lei*. The *lei* was later given to a loved one.]"[190]

When we love someone, we will fight inertia and work out ways to express and to cultivate this relationship. Who or what is worth fighting for in our lives? The people at work? A promotion? A bonus? Undoubtedly few will lie on their deathbeds bemoaning the fact that they could have worked more days in their lifetime. Yet, and y-e-t, many will sacrifice a meal with the family or a child's ballgame or theater performance for a business trip. Even at the last minute, many of us will sacrifice plans for family and self (not to mention God) for the sake of the company. Gotta do it. Sorry, honey. Operative values reveal themselves in our choices. We need to convert some of our energy from sacrificing for business travel, for example, to sacrificing for our relationship with God and with our family. What sacrifice it would take to choose to leave work abruptly for a spontaneous trip to the circus for the family. Or a weekend retreat, cultivating the inner life of the spirit. Out of the question? If we always do what we have always done, then we will always get what we have always gotten.

When approaching doctoral studies twenty years ago, I vividly remember praying to God: never allow me to sacrifice at the altar of the Ph.D. Over the years, I had witnessed countless sacrifice their marriages, health, playfulness, friendships, peace of mind, etc., in order to attain this coveted academic degree. Being a Jesuit, blessed with a good community of committed fellow believers and a regular prayer life, I did not imagine how tempting it

---

[190.] Ibid., p. 177, no. 1638.

would become to worship at the altar of the Ph.D. Of course we need to sacrifice a lot in order to obtain such a degree; but when some thing becomes so all important that God no longer remains central, who is the work for? Fighting for the degree did become a dog fight between myself and God. The Bible story about worshiping the golden calf[191] suddenly made more sense. What makes us loveable and worthwhile is not what we have but who we are in relation to God. Degrees do not give us love unless we fight for them with a loving spirit, not a driven, compulsive spirit. Fighting for a promotion, condominium, time-share property, a particular kind of car or house will not bring contentment unless the sacrifices required come out of a loving, freeing spirit. If the sacrifices become indiscriminate, disrespecting our limits and those of others, we will lose peace of mind and maybe relationships. We will find ourselves spinning wheels in the sand or snow and ice, unable to find traction because we lost our foundational relationships.

Sacrifices are not valuable in themselves. The context of the relationships makes all the difference in the world. In the first part of the ancient Hawaiian festival of Makahiki, the chief of each district (in addition to the *kahuna*) would presents gifts from himself and all the people to the image, to the god (Lono) who brought them prosperity and who caused these gifts to grow, these gifts to be plentiful.[192] We too need to restore our sacrifices in connection with God. Do we care enough to make sacrifices for more than our company and ourselves alone?

In relationships of significance, many of us get tempted to operate with an American 50-50 principle. I will do this much for

---

[191.] Exodus 20:4 and Acts of the Apostles 7:41.
[192.] Handy et al., Ancient Hawaiian Civilization, p. 65.

you and you will do this much for me. While this way of operating may serve business well, it will kill Christian living. Jesus on the cross is anything but 50-50. If God operated on this tit-for-tat principle, we would be dead meat. While not promoting that we become the doormat for the world by taking inadequate care of ourselves, Jesus modeled choices different from the priorities of the world. Calculated giving with strings attached will leave us with relationships as shallow as most business relationships. We reap what we sow, Jesus said.[193]

When we approach the altar, are we aware of its shape? If rectangular, the shape connotes a sarcophagus, a tomb, a coffin. Willingly Jesus sacrificed his one human lifetime to incarnate the gospel, so that he might salvage us from our human, messy predicament. Are we willing to put our bodies on the altar, to put our lives on the line to embody gospel living? If we choose to go the route of following Jesus, it will cost us as dearly as it cost him.

In the Prayer Over the Gifts for Epiphany we pray: "Lord, accept the offerings of your Church, not gold, frankincense and myrrh, but the sacrifice and food they symbolize: Jesus Christ, who is Lord forever and ever."[194]

In Eucharistic Prayer IV we pray that like Jesus we might be "a living sacrifice of praise."[195] These words do not constitute pious rhetoric alone. We must incarnate them as Jesus did. We must embody them within the flesh-and-blood relationships, ordinary circumstances of our lives. And in the Preface for Holy Men and

---

[193.] Galations .6 : 7.
[194.] The Sacramentary, p. 64.
[195.] Ibid., p. 559.

Women we pray that we too might "be the living sign of God's saving power."[196] To do so will require sacrifice.

During the "Lamb of God," the actions of breaking and pouring intend to evoke the meanings associated with the cost of sacrifice to live as Jesus. We pray that we may be willing to be **broken** in our faithfully caring for those God sends us and that we may be willing to be **poured out** in loving service as Jesus. For it is in restoring the breaking and pouring that we find life which satisfies and lasts.

[196.] Ibid., p. 513.

Part Five: Honoring Humility

In ancient Hawaii, certain individuals served the community by sounding the *pu* (blowing the conch shell). This symbolic gesture announced the arrival of the royalty (*ali'i*) and the inception of something major like a celebration. In the context of a Christian frame of reference, we trumpet the arrival of the reign of God, not ourselves. Building God's kingdom rivets the attention of the follower of Jesus more than establishing and trumpeting our own individual achievements. These become important only to the extent that our efforts are part of the building of the reign of God. Every week at Eucharist we pray: "...for the kingdom, the power and the glory are <u>yours</u>, now and forever."[197]

"E 'olu'olu i ka mea i loa'a.

Be contented with what one has."[198]

[197.] <u>The Sacramentary</u>, p. 562.
[198.] Pukui, <u>'Olelo: Proverbs</u>, p. 45, no. 367.

Via negativa offers one way to theologize. Presenting what we do not mean will clarify the area we examine. Being humble does not foster false humility, does not encourage the charade of pretending that we do not have something which we really possess. In fact, the opposite. Humility fosters the truth, no more and no less than the truth. Growing in humility does not promote developing an inferiority complex, actually believing that we are worth less than we really are. Surely a humble spirit does not embody a "beat me, beat me" attitude toward others, as if we are virtuous for becoming the whipping boy of the world.

The root meaning of the word humility is *humus*, Latin for earth. We need to learn how to walk on the earth and not pretend that we can walk several feet off the earth. The truth of the matter: we are a creature of earth, not the Creator.

"The foundation of the home in ancient Hawaii anchored in the relationship with God. They lived by prayer (*pule*)–when they got up in the morning, before and after meals, before and after and sometimes during work, before going to bed. *Ho' omanawa nui* (be humble) was part of family life in Hawaii of old."[199]

The relationships with the gods fostered respect and responsibility: who am I in relation to them and who am I not? "In general, the Hawaiian attitude toward *haipule* or prayerfulness was one of humility, deference and reverence...even in the most intimate relationship with *'aumakua* (ancestral family gods), one prays with fervor and urgency, never taking the gods for granted– and certainly never insulting them."[200]

[199.] Personal interview with Zita Leimomi Mo'okini Lum 14 January 2004.

[200.] Kanahele, Ku Kanaka Stand Tall, p. 126-127.

During the latter half of 1982, a series of four *Ho'okanaka* Training Workshops occurred in order to help the hundred participants to clarify their values and goals which help them realize their "Hawaiianness." Of the twenty-five values the group identified, they named humility (*ha'aha'a*) as one which continues to characterize the best of a Hawaiian.[201]

God directs the unfolding drama of our lives. Chosen by God, we are called to take a unique part in the production which no one else plays. Surely we play together and interact with others in the drama. Often during these days in this country, it seems we rebel against the roles we receive. We want a different part, a bigger part, a more significant part—from our point of view. Only we do not direct the play. As the opening Hawaiian proverb indicated, we need to learn how to content ourselves with our part, even though we may bristle at needing to play a "bit part" and find ourselves chaffing at the bit for a more glitzy role. If we follow the lead of the American cultures uncritically and passively, often we will let ourselves be swept up into a lust for power and prestige and money and what it buys. Of course, the specific shape this takes depends upon the frames of reference of the individual cultures of our country.

Being content with who we are and what we have does not equate with laziness. Industriously we can work with the gifts God gives us as we decipher the directions God invites, as we respond to these gifts. Arrogantly imagining that we have more gifts than are there can incline us to become pushy or driven. We have real limits. At worst we can embody the Peter Principle, passively allowing or actively seeking promotion beyond our level of competence. In such circumstances, others become miserable and so do we. Similar to

---

[201.] Ibid., p. 18-21.

wearing shoes that just do not fit, we find ourselves wincing from the dissatisfaction of trying to wear something which does not suit us. Sometimes others know this before we do, especially if our self-knowledge is limited in notable ways. <u>Good</u> friends will tell us if they sense we are willing to listen. We can ask them what they think about our reaching for this promotion or this job. For example, we could say: Do you think this move is healthy for me (the next best step, of God) or do you think I am trying to become something I cannot be?

Praying with the words of the psalmist can honor the humble spirit growing within us, even if this spirit seems like the smallest mustard seed: "Lord, my heart is not proud; nor are my eyes haughty. I do not busy myself with great matters, with things too sublime for me."[202]

Happiness is not having everything we want. Rather, it comes from wanting what we have and embracing it with passion. What we have is always a blend of blessings and curses, positives and negatives, crowns and crosses. Developing a sense of contentment with our gifts presumes we become aware of them, appreciate them as gifts, enjoy them and share them with others.

The Christian scriptures challenge our tendency to look arrogantly at others' ways of thinking, feeling, operating. St. Paul exhorts the believers at Philippi: "...humbly regard others as more important than yourselves."[203]

During my rookie years as a helping professional, I recognize (with embarrassment in more recent years) how I would share stories about the amazing ways I witnessed people being helped in my

---

[202.] Psalm 131.
[203.] Philippians 2:3.

presence. With the best of intentions, I found myself astounded by the ways others reached for my gifts and found them helpful. Surely my hackles would have stood up if someone would have tried to tell me about insecurity in the carrying of my gifts. I felt confident, or so I thought. With the privilege of graced hindsight, now I can see the short-sightedness of saying: can you believe *I* was instrumental in this situation?

God has enabled me to see with a new lens, with deeper faith. Yes, I was instrumental. For whom is this a surprise? For the one who does not know and have a developed sense of the gifts I brought to the situation. The REAL story puts the emphasis on the word instrumental. A surgeon can operate with refined instruments, but the best instruments in the world without a skilled surgeon work no wonders. The big news which amazes me more now than as a rookie: **God** works with us. Is not this amazing? Awesome? The more aware we are of God operating in every situation, the more humble we become. The real good news is that the story is bigger than our myopic view allows us to perceive and to understand fully. Can we carry our skewed vision with a measure of humor? On good days. Taking it all too seriously does not help. We are all human. And we need to let God be God, entrusting our failures into the sea of God's compassionate merciful love and recognizing that our short-sightedness can be transformed by God's power in time.

Sometimes we get in over our heads, and we realize (on hindsight usually) that we have over-stepped our bounds. Even with the best of intentions, we can discover ourselves endeavoring to do more than we can with peace of mind. While keeping our word after committing ourselves to a goal or to a person remains a value, so too does humbly recognizing that we have over-estimated our limits. We need to keep growing in self-knowledge to the point that we can say "no" when others ask us to perform functions beyond our scope–either we are incapable of fulfilling the request at all or at this time, given other outstanding commitments. People have a right to request, but no one has a right to demand. Only God can be "on call" twenty-four hours a day, seven days a week.[204] Even a parent needs to monitor his or her limits. There is only one God, and less there be any confusion, none of us is the One. We could do well to reflect upon the clear differentiation of John the Baptist: I am not the One...there is another the strap of whose sandals I am not worthy to untie.[205]

Evil can hide under the guise of good, as Ignatius Loyola helped us understand.[206] What   could possibly be wrong with us helping this needy person with this request? It looks noble to others and perhaps to ourselves; but when we scratch the surface with a prayerful depth perception,[207] God can give us the graced insight to realize we *should not* say "yes" to one more thing right now without disrespecting our limits. Part of integrity involves respecting our limits. With an interpretation only a mother could give, my Mom would say: you are so like your father, your heart is as big as your body. I would feel noble and self-justified for my over-extension until one day God provided the graced insight to see the half-truth in my all too familiar way of operating. Another true part of the picture came to light: quit playing God! Only God has boundless energy and needs no time to sleep and to recoup. Only God can "do it all." Really and truly, we can only love others as we love ourselves.[208]

[204.] See T. Jerome Overbeck, S.J., "The Workaholic" in <u>Psychology: A Journal of Human Behavior, Vol. 13, No.3, 1976.</u>

[205.] Luke 3:15-16.

[206.] St. Ignatius Loyola, "Guidelines for the Discernment of Spirits: Thirteenth Rule" [326] in <u>The Spiritual Exercises</u>.

[207.] As Ignatius mentions, sometimes we need the help of others to see. Perhaps a spiritual director, a good mentor and a friend can help us achieve this prayerful depth perception.

[208.] Leviticus 19:18, Matthew 19:19 and 22:39, Mark 12:31, Romans 13:9, Galatians 5:14, James 2:8.

While the intentions may be pure, the proverbial road to hell is paved with them. Bottom line: let God be God and become more content with doing our little part in letting God build the kingdom with or without us. God saves the world, not us. As the late and beloved bishop and martyr Oscar Romero once said: God needs more ministers and not messiahs.

Sometimes we handle our gifts in ways unbefitting a follower of Jesus. For example, even when we have a portion of the truth within our sights, we can speak it in an off-putting way which those around us might think (if not say) is arrogant, anything but humble. Speaking the truth in love[209] honors the Lord who alone knows it all and acknowledges the fact that we see bits and pieces, in a mirror darkly. Surely some of us become more knowledgeable than others in given areas, but each of us brings something to the table. The most uneducated person in the world can help a scholar learn something that he never knew or has forgotten. The best professors learn from their students each semester. When someone *thinks* he or she knows more than they do, how tempting it can be to fire back in arrogant and angry ways which disrespect the other individual. Often the person with much room to grow in humility is one of the last persons to realize that others have tip-toed around him or her for years, scared that they might get clobbered by the arrogant way the knowledge gets delivered.

While examining Hawaiian culture of old, how saddening to find foreign-born followers of Jesus as well as some contemporary Hawaiians referring to the indigenous people as savages and heathens. In discussing attitudes toward ancient Hawaiians who believed in many gods, George Hu'eu Sanford Kanahele addressed the sense of disbelief or even shame about the ancestors' ways of

---

209. Psalm 15:2, Zechariah 8:16, Ephesians 4:25.

believing. He found it understandable when people do not comprehend the subject, "but it also betrays the usual arrogance of persons who think, whether consciously or unconsciously, that somehow they are superior."[210]

We need to be careful with what we know and how we speak about it, listening with care in a humble spirit for what others have to teach us about the God who plays in ten thousand faces. We try to foster good judgment as a virtue and to eradicate judgmentalism as a vice. We risk a divide when we assess something and experience someone as not only different but also out of bounds. Is there any truth in the other? How we differ can make all the difference in the world. For example, Drs. Pukui, Haertig and Lee described the reaction of many Hawaiians of old when someone refused to eat food that was offered. The indigenous response would be: "He is *ho'okano*. He is stuck up–he thinks he is too good for us and our food...need(ing) a lesson in how Hawaiians see eating and how to respond when offered food...take a bite or two or a cup of coffee, something."[211] While resisting the temptation to adopt cultural relativism, and simply ape the mindless response of "whatever," we must be alert to and respectful of the situation of others. We can become preoccupied with ourselves and the correctness of our message and overlook whether others can receive in the way we are putting it. The primary action is in the listener. We might also humbly search for something–even a smidgeon of truth in anything they say or do–which unites us. How self-righteousness can infect how we convey what we know.

Ethnobotonist and phycologist at the University of Hawaii, Dr. Isabella Aiona Abbot exemplifies a way other than an arrogant,

---

[210] Kanahele, Ku Kanaka Stand Tall, p. 71.
[211] Pukui, Haertig and Lee, Nana I Ke Kumu (Look to the Source), Vol 1, p. 8.

in-your-face approach. "Being Hawaiian to me, is a softer approach. It isn't that you don't see things the way a scientifically trained person would, but you don't hit it head on. When you're talking to Hawaiians it's the same thing–you don't hit a person head on. You never in your life would say: 'you've got it all wrong. I don't believe you.' You might think that, but you go around the back door, talk story. Fifteen minutes later you've diffused what they have said, but you have never told them to their face: 'you're wrong.'"[212]

Again, our approach to others should not become equivocating, talking out of both sides of our mouth. Rather, we reach for other ways of presenting our particular angle on a truth we have appropriated. Being attentive to the needs of others need not denigrate into spin-doctoring with or without an arrogant smirk.

We can exercise our spirit of humility in worship–one place we honor this virtue. Believers gather to remember and to celebrate on a regular basis that God is always the One to serve, not our ego. How easily our contemporary culture cultivates an attitude aptly described this way: "It's all about me." Without realizing it, self-centered filters creep into our way of perceiving. Where can we go to see from another perspective, to imagine what life would be like if we enfleshed the message of Jesus? In Christian worship we can imagine saying and doing things differently. We can ask probing questions, e.g., how else could we approach this situation? Would Jesus approach it this way? In light of the Sermon on the Mount, for instance, would Jesus rephrase what I want to say? The scriptures inspire, breathe new life into us–a fresh approach which enlivens both us and, indirectly, those with whom we interact.

[212.] Harden, ed., <u>Voices of Wisdom</u>, p. 26.

The Hawaiians of old found comparable value in religious ritual as they approached their lives in light of the divine and enacting the right relationships with the gods: "...if ritual means imitating the acts of the gods, then that is precisely what we must do...changing or tampering with a divine model would be like saying 'we can do better than the gods.' Besides the value of excellence, desire to do the best possible job, Hawaiians of old would respect and reverence the details of religious rituals."[213] Being cavalier in one's relationship with the divine found throughout life in ancient Hawaii would have been unthinkable. Their whole culture discouraged carrying oneself with an arrogant attitude.[214] Unlike the brashness and permissiveness of today, in the Hawaii of old, young and old Islanders alike would worship daily with deference to the gods who brought them life, prosperity, healing—everything they had. This deferential attitude toward the gods impacted the peoples' attitudes toward each other.

By their very nature, rituals are repeated actions. We exercise our spirit of humility by choosing actions which suit us in our time and place for cultivating this virtue which eludes many in our American culture these days.

M.J. Harden describes one such ritual gesture in Hawaii of old: "He picks a large *ti* leaf, a plant sacred to the god Lono, and puts it on his forehead as a headband. This helps me release my inner feelings...it helps me to be humble."[215]

The *ho'oponopono* ritual of old Hawaii required a humble spirit. The wisdom figure of the family would assemble the entire

---

[213.] Kanahele, <u>Ku Kanaka Stand Tall</u>, p. 112.

[214.] Personal interview with Tutu Pat (Maka) Bacon, Bishop Museum, Honolulu 18 November 2003.

[215.] Harden, <u>Voices of Wisdom</u>, p. 35.

immediate family and, after prayer to the family ancestral gods (*'aumakuas*) invite quiet reflection and conversation about whatever misunderstandings and offenses the family experienced as debilitating. The ritual required confidentiality and respect. People achieved reconciliation only by speaking the truth, even if it hurt, in the hopes of achieving right relationships in the family. How many times do we live with the proverbial elephant in the room rather than risk such a ritual at home or at work, or in a supposed friendship? Often we tend to "play it safe," talk about anything except sex, politics and religion–anything that really matters. Approaching a reconciliation ritual such as *ho'oponopono* with a humble and contrite heart is precisely how the Lord asks us to approach him.[216]

Kahuna nui Momi Mo'okini Lum described another form of *ho'oponopono* which expresses and cultivates a humble spirit, when some resentment has festered between two people. They go to the ocean together and each one picks up from the water's edge a bunch of special seaweed called *limu kala*. While holding the seaweed, each verbalizes a prayerful asking of forgiveness from God and from the other who was hurt. After the prayer from a humble and contrite heart, the person releases the seaweed back into the ocean of God's forgiving mercy.[217]

We need to work toward communicating with God and others in this spirit of humility. President of Kamehameha Schools/Bernice Pauahi Bishop Estates' Board of Trustees and former Big Island State senator, Richard Ka'ilihiwa Lyman rooted his reflection upon our ways of living together in light of valuable lessons learned from the Hawaiian past. "Our culture was based on faith, land and nature. It was not written, but it was established and

---

[216.] Psalm 51:17.
[217.] Personal interview with Zita Leimomi Mo'okini Lum 10 December 2003.

was perpetuated by the example of people living and working together. This is not impossible even today if we are fair and willing to sit down and communicate with each other–not only to talk but to listen–in the sense of *ho'oponopono*. The end result will be good for all of us, not only for Hawaiians, but for America and the world because it is healthy, especially now. If we cannot admit to wrongs at home, how can we expect people to support us when we oppose actions of others elsewhere?"[218]

When functioning in our world from a shaky position (when we feel insecure about whether we have much to offer), but especially when we approach others from a position of strength (confident that we have much to offer), we would do well to make explicit to ourselves what we bring to the table. No one is good at everything; but we each have some things to offer. Then, and most important of all, look at these as gifts of God–not primarily what I have, but what God gives to me. Oh the difference between an egocentric lens and one of faith. The remembering and celebrating of our gifts will not induce an egotistical attitude, but a humble one because these are gifts. Gratitude and humility will grow and arrogance will diminish as we stay finely tuned to our embarrassment of riches. Rather than giving in to clubbing others with our strengths, preying on their weaknesses, a humble spirit will gestate within us. The centuries' old wisdom of St. Francis de Sales rings true as ever: there is nothing more powerful than real gentleness and nothing more gentle than real strength.[219] Meek but not weak.

Hawaiian Richard Ka'ilihiwa Lyman offers a fine example of incarnating humility when he writes: "We must never forget our

---

[218.] Richard Ka'ilihiwa Lyman, *Mea Ho'omana'o: My Thoughts*. Honolulu: The Estate of Richard Lyman, 1995, p. 38.
[219.] St. Francis de Sales

roots...we must perpetuate all the best things that we have inherited from our ancestors and at the same time use the best things that we have absorbed and learned from our new arrivals from other lands. In learning from others we should be *ma'a* (knowing thoroughly, habituated, experienced)[220] to their ways as they are to ours."[221]

The world gets smaller all the time, meaning we can choose to learn more and more about our global village. Why bother? Precisely because we can learn so much from each other. We need to learn how to approach others with greater respect and reverence. While eager to learn more, we can approach especially others considerably different from us with attentiveness to their readiness to relay the gifts in their storehouse. Obviously it would be arrogant to assume to know all about that storehouse or to attempt to barge inside. We can ask, but it does not help to force.

On occasion, *Kahuna nui* Momi Mo'okini Lum verbalizes a Hawaiian proverb germane to the issue of developing a humble spirit.

> " *'A'ole 'oe, no keia halau*
> *no laila 'a'ole no 'oe i ike i ko'u po'opo'o.*

> You are not of my house,
> so, you know not the secret of its closets."[222]

---

[220]. Mary Kawena Pukui and Samuel H. Elbert, Hawaiian Dictionary: Hawaiian-English, English-Hawaiian (Revised and Enlarged Edition). Honolulu: University of Hawaii Press, p. 217.

[221]. Lyman, *Mea Ho'omanao: My Thoughts*, p. 2.

[222]. Lecture by Zita Leimomi Mo'okini Lum at the University of Hawaii, 26 August 1968.

We must respect the interior life of each person and family and culture. As we approach others, let alone ourselves, may we humbly honor the mystery present in us all and in each one of us.

Part Six: Practicing Patience

" 'A 'ohe hua o ka mai'a ka la ho'okahi

Bananas do not fruit in a single day.

[A retort to an impatient person.]"[223]

Often within the Hawaiian language, especially in these proverbs, metaphors bear the meaning. We reflect upon practicing the art of patience in a contemporary American culture usually driven by the fast lane, the quick fix, fast food, instant winners, quick service, one-stop shopping. We hanker for short cuts to obtain short-term profits. What works in business with a market-driven economy may yield impressive results fiscally, but bankrupt us spiritually. In other words, running our spiritual lives like our business lives can jeopardize our interior lives. We need to learn the lesson of the oak tree: it grew sturdy and tall because it grew slowly and well. [224] Figuring out the next best step and patiently practicing

---

[223.] Pukui, *'Olelo: Proverbs*, p. 18, no. 143.
[224.] Wilfred Peterson, "Slow Me Down, Lord" in <u>Adventures in the Art of Living</u>. New York: Simon and Schuster, 1968.

this graced insight may bear fruit which lasts. Over time and with God's grace, a good tree will bear good fruit. As Jesus said, we know a good tree by the fruit it bears.[225]

In *Nana I Ke Kumu* (Look to the Source), Mary Kawena Pukui described how a thoughtful Hawaiian hoped his child would become a mentally and emotionally mature person (*kanaka makua*): "He does not jump into things...he takes responsibility."[226] Achieving consequences of significance requires patience as well as sacrifice. How tempting in this part of the world today to flit from one thing or person to another rather than to commit. The end result of dabbling produces a fruit different from responsible commitment.

The style of living we choose can pre-empt us from genuinely connecting with others, including God, and even ourselves. Quoting Abraham Fornander's 1917 Hawaiian Antiquities and Folklore (Vol. IV), the Office of Hawaiian Affairs described how hospitality (*ho'okipa*) called for slowing down:

"*...Kaha loa mai o Eleio hele make alanui, kahea mai o Kaniakaniaula , 'Ea! Hele*
loa no ka, aole ka e olelo mai. A lohe o Eleio i keia leo, huli aku la i a aloha aku la.
...Eleio passed right on by the pathway, Kaniakaniaula called out, 'Say! You are going so fast you won't even greet me.'
Eleio heard her and he turned around to greet her.

[This was the story about a runner and messenger named Eleio. As he traveled on the pathway to Kaupo on Maui, he passed a woman named Kaniakaniaula.][227]

---

225. Matthew 7:17 and Luke 6:43.
226. Pukui, Haertig and Lee, Nana I Ke Kumu (Look to the Source), Vol. I, p. 118.

We can be too busy, too rushed for our own good. Tempering a hurried pace by practicing patience, we can attend to relationships with ourselves (what the tenor of our inner life is like), as well as to our relationships with God and others. Sometimes like Eleio we do not notice because we hurry to check another item off our "to do" list. We have set an agenda with little or no room for the unexpected. We can get preoccupied with the item itself and lose touch with our own inner life as well as the tenor of the lives of others. It takes time and patience to connect on more than superficial levels. We could approach even perfunctory tasks in a spirit which would not sap our energy. To do so may require a sacrifice of completing some tasks as quickly for the sake of salvaging more than sanity. The goal of the day (not to mention our life) ought to be more than survival, gutting it out, getting through the list.

Hawaiians will speak about patience in a variety of ways. They might reference *ho'omanawanui*, *ho'omalie*, *ho'omalu* and *ahonui*. They would use each in a little different context, expressing nuances deserving further reflection.

Ho'omanawanui references us "to be patient; to be long-suffering, to continue steadfast; to bear up against difficulties; to be persevering."[228] When a person or situation tries our patience, we need to have roots or the difficulty of the experience will blow us away. One of the old Hawaiian proverbs expresses this about someone incapable of sustaining patient endurance.

---

227. *Ho'okipa: Hawaiian Hospitality*. Honolulu: Office of Hawaiian Affairs, 1988, p. 6.
228. Lorrin Andrews, A Dcitionary of the Hawaiian Language. Waipahu, HI: Island Heritage Publishing, 2003, p. 386.

"He pu hala a'a kiolea.

A hala tree with thin, hanging roots.

[Said of one who is not strong, like a tree with aerial roots that are not yet imbedded in the earth.]"[229]

We must sink our roots in the relationships of significance, as the Bible tells us. If we start by deepening our relationship with God, and nourish these roots regularly at the Table of the Word and the Table of the Eucharist, we will have the inner strength to live through these storms.

"He lala kamahele no ka la'au
ku i ka pali.

A far-reaching branch of the tree
standing on the cliff.

[Meaning. A boast of a strong person who, like the tree on the cliff, can withstand gales and pouring rain.][230]

Like the parable of Jesus contrasting the construction of a house on sand and one built on rock, this Hawaiian proverb praises the patient endurance of a strong person who can manage in spite of unfriendly winds which prove devastating to some others. Jesus says part of the story involves not merely "talking a good game," but especially walking the walk. Do we act on the word of God and not merely think about it or talk about it occasionally? More likely, putting the Word into action occurs when the roots of our

---

[229.] Pukui, *'Olelo: Proverbs*, p. 99, no. 923.
[230.] Ibid., p. 79, no. 717.

relationships with God and people of God run deeply through regular spiritual exercise. Rugged individualism seems less helpful. The "buddy system" seems a better approach. The connection with the Lord and people of faith can develop such a tensile strength that we can weather the storms together with the Lord and each other.

> *"He ʻaʻaliʻi ku makani mai au;*
> *ʻaʻohe makani nana e kulaʻi.*

> I am a wind-resisting *ʻaʻaliʻi*;
> no gale can push me over.

[A boast meaning 'I can hold my own even in the face of difficulties.' The ʻaʻaliʻI bush can stand the worst of gales, twisting and bending but seldom breaking off or falling over.]"[231]

For a follower of Jesus, the strength to patiently persevere comes from the Lord. If we boast about anything, it goes to the Lord, as St. Paul reminds us.[232] Our patiently bearing with our weakness becomes the vehicle for God to reveal clearly that it is his power which sets us free.[233] We do not save ourselves, pull ourselves up by our own bootstraps. This mentality can go against our American grain of self-sufficiency and our illusion of having more control than we have.

The complexities of our lives require a measure of flexibility in the face of mounting difficulties. To get brittle does no good. Part of patience includes being flexible enough to acknowledge our limits and adjust before we hit the wall. In order to remain patient and long-suffering, we need to take adequate care of ourselves for

---

[231.] Pukui, *ʻOlelo: Proverbs*, p. 60, no. 507.
[232.] 1 Corinthians 1: 31 and Romans 11: 18.
[233.] 2 Corinthians 12: 9.

the long haul. Think marathon not sprint when patiently adapting to the cost of faithful love. How easily we talk about loving someone or some group forever. It takes God's grace of patience to actually love them for better or worse, in sickness as well as in health, as long as we both shall live. *Mutatis mutandi*, the gracefulness of God enables us to stay light on our feet as we try to care faithfully for our children, our family, our friends, our selves. A tempting alternative for us: throw in the towel... forget it...no one and nothing is worth this much effort.

Ho'omalie references us "to be calm, quiet, still, gentle."[234] Easier said than done when we feel caught in a whirlwind, wondering how this mess will eventually work out. It is hard for us to wait. Reflect upon how most of us react to rush-hour traffic, waiting for an elevator, waiting for a promotion or a raise, waiting for the right time to say something, waiting for an answer to a prayer.

"Hohonu no ke kawa.

A deep diving place indeed.

[A topic that requires deep thinking.]"[235]

Some situations require us to think deeply. We might prefer a quick resolution, but we need patience to plumb the depths, to see the patterns, to look for the signs, to sense the interior movements. We need to pray, *pule* as the Hawaiians of old would say, and wait patiently–with a measure of calm–for the Lord to reveal the next best step.

---

234. Andrews, <u>Dictionary of Hawaiian Language</u>, p. 380.
235. Pukui, <u>'Olelo: Proverbs</u>, p. 109, no.1022.

Ho'omalu means "to bless; to comfort; to make comfortable."[236] The wise leader of a *ho'oponopono* ritual[237] would invoke *ho'omalu* and also in other situations. For example, in Hawaii of old *ho'omalu* was decreed to ensure quiet during important religious rituals. "*Ho'omalu* recognizes man's need for calm and prayerful contemplation."[238] Part of waiting patiently involves an interior calm, making room for gentle probing and contemplation. Sometimes we need to wait, whether we like it or not, and allow the Lord (sometimes in the quiet of our individual hearts and other times through others) to bless us with an interior settling. It seems analogous to stirring up the bottom of a lake, when all the sediment mixes with the water. This blurs our vision. We cannot see clearly so we need to wait patiently for it all to settle. Ignatius Loyola himself cautioned people not to make decisions (especially important ones) out of a disturbed interior context.[239]

When any of us finds ourselves in stormy circumstances, we appreciate a safe port in the storm. This restores hope and much-needed anchoring in whom and what matters most: God and the gospel. In Eucharistic Prayer for Masses for Various Needs and Occasions IV: God Guides the Church on the Way of Salvation, we pray: "...may we follow your paths in faith and hope and radiate our joy and trust to all the world."[240] As followers of Jesus we want to

---

236. Andrews, <u>Dictionary of Hawaiian Language</u>, p. 382.

237. As described earlier, this formal ritual gathered all the family members for mutual confession of wrongs, forgiveness and restoration of good relationships. See Pukui, Haertig and Lee, <u>Nana I Ke Kumu (Look to the Source)</u>, Vol. I, p. 95.

238. Ibid., p. 77.

239. St. Ignatius Loyola "Guidelines for the Discernment of Spirits" in <u>The Spiritual Exercises</u>, no. 318.

240. "God Guides the Church on the Way to Salvation" in <u>Eucharistic Prayer for Masses for Various Needs and Occasions</u>. New Jersey: Catholic Book Publishing Co., 1996, p. 33.

be one who can *ho'omalu*, bring a sense of calm and stabilizing. This provides a much-needed service to someone trying to navigate treacherous waters, especially when significant decisions loom.

At times in our lives we all wrestle with the Lord for the control panel.[241] A big part of us needs to learn that we do not have full control. Life is much more mysterious than we usually realize. Especially in our part of the world at this time, we live with this grand illusion that we have so much control. Many variables exist beyond our control. We can work industriously and feel we deserve a given outcome. We can line up everything as best we can to achieve a desired objective by the time of *our* choosing and be disgruntled to discover some facet will not work as we had planned. As some say, if you want to see God laugh, make plans. Several points here deserve reflection: (1) if our plan is not "of God" it will not last, and (2) only in *God's* time will the direction emerge and plans materialize.

We need patience to wait on the Lord–cues from the Lord that now is the time to make a move. Until this time, we can do something significant, i.e., patiently pray and wait. Perhaps we can *pai pai* the waters (ruffle the surface water to attract the fish)[242] when it seems timely; but if the Lord does not bless the effort, nothing lasting will come of it. As the psalmist reveals: if the Lord does not build a house, then in vain do the builders labor.[243] We need the gift of patience to be able to sit tight and remain calm. Especially when we want a quick and easy resolution, whatever and whoever shelters us and periodically protects us from the turbulence along the way

---

[241.] Genesis 32: 24.

[242.] An ancient Hawaiian metaphorical expression which *kahuna nui* Leimomi Mo'okini Lum uses periodically.

[243.] Psalm 127: 1.

enable us to filter out the extraneous matter and wait for clearer signs from the Lord.

Ahonui references us "to be patient, gentle, kind."[244] Often what tries our patience emanates from a place close to home–where we would least expect. This Hawaiian proverb alerts those willing to learn this painful lesson.

" *'A ole make ka wa'a i ka 'ale o*
waho, aia no i ka 'ale o loco.

A canoe is not swamped by the
billows of the ocean, but by the
billows near land.

[Trouble often comes from one's own people rather than from outsiders.]"[245]

Jesus spoke a similar message when he said a prophet is not accepted in his own native territory.[246] If we are not careful, taking a hit from somewhere close to home hurts the most and can undercut our ability to be patient, gentle, kind. Unfortunately, some of the unkindest cuts of all come from ourselves. Hence the origin of the expression, we are our own worst enemy. This is not a complement. Some of us would not treat strangers the way we treat ourselves. In such cases, we would give evidence of unkindness, harshness and impatience–all self-directed.

After working with a psychiatrist in Oakland, California, to facilitate a group therapy session, he noticed my unsettledness

244. Andrews, Dictionary of Hawaiian Language, p. 38.
245. Pukui, 'Olelo: Proverbs, p. 27, no. 229.
246. Luke 4:24.

toward the end of the session. After everyone left, he inquired about the cause. I expressed my chagrin about how poorly some people treat themselves. He smiled and asked a probing question: when all the people you help leave the university, who are you left with–your own best friend or your own worst enemy? Did this question provoke considerable thought and prayer for years. I knew that I was not my own worst enemy (like I had noticed in many patients with severe personality disorders), but I also realized I could learn how to be a much better friend to myself.

Over the years we can learn ways to be good and kind to ourselves, find ways to gentle the hard sides of ourselves. We can learn to cultivate a patient living with the real, sometimes harsh and disconcerting variables. We can also learn how to ask trusted family and friends for what we need, especially when those close to home (including ourselves) devastate us.

Whether directed at ourselves or at others, if we selectively hone in on faults, we will find plenty. For example, we could become intolerant about the hypocrisy within us or in others and let frustration (a form of anger) fester. We could get very demanding, allowing little or no room for error.

"E moni i ke koko o ka
inaina, 'umi ka hanu o ka
ho'omanawanui.

Swallow the blood of wrath and
hold the breath of patience."[247]

---

247. Pukui, *'Olelo: Proverbs*, p. 64, no. 353.

How can we find scrappy ways to gentle the sides of us which become demanding, impatient with imperfection?

We would do well to avoid the extremes of passivity and of pushing too hard. Some in the Buddhist tradition warn against attempting to push the river, an impossibility and a waste of energy. Our Bible offers an analogous message: there is a time for everything under heaven.[248] At the opposite extreme lies passivity, not lifting a finger to do anything–consult, pray, gather data, play with alternatives, etc.

"Po'e ho'ohaha pa'akai.

Salt gathers.

[A derogatory expression for people who do nothing that requires courage or stamina. Salt-gathering is an easy task that even a child can do.]"[249]

We can muster the intestinal fortitude to take initiative. At some point in our lives we need to take our gifts and claim responsibility for how we use them. Blaming others and ourselves gets old and goes nowhere. We need to acknowledge what we have and have done with our gifts, accept responsibility for our choices in all of that, ask forgiveness where necessary, *and move on.* We can choose disciplined action to move beyond inertia.

[248.] Ecclesiastes 3: 1.
[249.] Pukui, *'Olelo: Proverbs,* p. 292, no. 2664.

The art of navigating tricky interior waters requires an avoidance of extremes. Sometimes the best course of action could be described as "steady as she goes."

"Pa'a 'ia iho i ka hoe uli i 'ole
e ika i ke ko'a.

Hold the steering paddle steady to
keep from striking the rock.

[Hold on; don't let yourself get into trouble.]"[250]

So, let us wait for the Lord–alone and with others. Often in prayer together God enables us to recover our lens of faith and find the reward of patient waiting. "The eyes of those who have sight will not be closed. The ears of those who have hearing will listen."[251]

"Ua ahu ka imu, e lawalu ka i'a.

The oven is ready, let the fish
wrapped in *ti* leaves be cooked.

[All preparations have been made; now let us proceed with the work.]"[252]

As we proceed with the work of building the reign of God, may we do so with a renewed sense of purpose. Some days we may feel like we are only a "piece of work," rather than a work in progress. Give our Lord the benefit of the doubt that God knows what is best for us and has not given up on us. Yes, we know a good

---

[250.] Ibid., p. 281, no. 2554.
[251.] Isaiah 32:3.
[252.] Pukui, 'Olelo: Proverbs, p. 305, no. 2768.

tree by the fruit it bears.[253]   We can begin again with what God provides for us and watch for fruitful results.

"He puko 'a kani 'aina.

A coral reef that grows into an island.

[A person beginning in a small way gains steadily until he becomes firmly established.]"[254]

Is this not the sense of Jesus' parable about the smallest of all the seeds (mustard seed) growing into a tree big enough for many to nest?[255] God provides us with the mustard seed of faith and God can grow this seed in ways which astound us.

Kahuna nui Momi Mo'okini Lum quotes an ancient Hawaiian proverb which calls people to take responsibility for our choices:

"Mai holo pai kino
mai holo pa!

You can lead a body where you want it to go, but you cannot make it do what you want."[256]

The sense of this expression resembles our mainland American proverb about leading a horse to water, but we cannot force him to drink.   Hopefully at some point we decide which

---

[253.] Matthew 7:17 and Luke 6: 43.

[254.] Pukui, *'Oleleo: Proverbs*, p. 100, no. 932.

[255.] Matthew 17:20, Luke 13:19 and Luke 17:6.

[256.] Personal interview with Zita Leimomi Mo'okini Lum 2 January 2004.

watering holes provide water worth drinking deeply. The community of faith encourages us to drink deeply from the interior well containing the water which truly satisfies.[257]

In the Eucharistic Prayer, "God Guides the Church on the Way to Salvation," we pray with whole heart and soul and body, "we proclaim the work of your love."[258] If we approach anyone or anything with less than the "work of your love," then it remains only a piece of work. It will not last, nor will it satisfy.

We keep our eyes on the Lord as we choose our next best step, praying along with the psalmist: "The eyes of all look hopefully to you, who give them their food in due season."[259]

---

[257] John 4: 14.

[258] "Eucharistic Prayer II: God Guides the Church on the Way to Salvation" in Eucharistic Prayers for Masses for Various Needs and Occasions. New Jersey: Catholic Book Publishing Co., 1996, p. 33.

[259] Psalm 145: 15.

EPILOGUE

Often when we live in the middle of an experience, we do not see clearly what occurs and what meanings the experience holds for us. Foresight remains even more oblique, and if we ever find someone blessed with exceptional foresight, we ought to draft in their presence and see if we can glean insights into their methods. And while seeing and understanding in the present moment and even more in the future can elude us, hindsight can sometimes offer clearer vision. While the expression "hindsight is 20-20" seems to overstate the case, still often we see more when we reflect upon our experiences. If God blesses us with the lens of faith and we use the gift, we can look back over our experiences and see the hand of God there.

With the lens of faith, on hindsight, I believe this research project reveals the providence of God. Look at the series of events that occurred:

- Of all the students I taught and lived with in the student residence hall nearly thirty years ago at Santa Clara University, how amazing that I would meet the granddaughter of the *kahuna nui* of the major line of the indigenous Hawaiian religion.

- Of the thousands of students we faculty meet each year, we become friends and stay friends with a small number.

- The granddaughter invited me to come to Hawaii in 1976 to help her celebrate her marriage. During the wedding celebration, and while I worked several weeks at a nearby parish, I got to know "grandpa," *kahuna nui*. Often we "talked story" on the porch (*lanai*).

- In the context of an extraordinarily blessed experience that summer of 1976, grandpa gave me my two Hawaiian names.[260] He died several months later.

- My Hawaiian friend and her family kept contact all these years and her mother's role as high priestess (*kahuna nui*) unfolded for the last thirty-seven years.

This sound sleeper who almost never awakens in the middle of the night, awoke clear as a bell during my annual eight-day silent retreat and said aloud: Hawaii. Only after many months of prayer and reflection alone and with my spiritual director and friends, did I even connect this experience with a possibility for this sabbatical. My last sabbatical research project studied ancient baptismal fonts in North Africa, the Middle East and Europe. Eventually I presented two options for sabbatical to my Jesuit Provincial who approved this option, the one to which I was mostly drawn.

A number of confirming experiences during my year here in the Islands brought such consolation and a blessed experiential base which revealed more of the mystery of this field of study. An embarrassment of riches.

All accidental? Mere happenstance, luck of the draw? I do not think so. I believe this research project was providential. Surely it helped me understand and appreciate more about our interior life of the spirit, and how worship with others and alone plays into growing interiorly. Hopefully others will profit from this research, starting with those I teach and for whom I preach; but hopefully many others as well.

[260.] A description of this experience can be found in the Foreword of this book.

As I said in the Introduction, this work does not offer a detailed, scientific, in-depth presentation of ancient Hawaii. Rather, we have reflected upon some of the emphases of the contemporary Mo'okini *kahuna nui* (who endeavors to preserve the best of the ancient Hawaiian past and to adapt it to the present) and the perspectives of this contemporary American Catholic-Jesuit-priest-professor of theology and of counseling psychology.

A wide variety of cultures and subcultures exist within Hawaii today as well as within the mainland of the United States of America. The generalizations of this book attempt to articulate some of the predominant confluences of cultural and religious vectors within Hawaii and the mainland. If this study opened my understanding and imagination to anything, surely it revealed the depth of this rich religious culture of Hawaii. The wisdom (*ike*) of the Hawaiian tradition can teach much to someone open and eager for learning. From the point of view of this author, much more remains to explore and to compare with the best of our Catholic tradition. What a worthwhile adventure: how to present some of the best of the past faithfully and yet connect it to the present time and place. Being a "bridge-person" opened an exciting journey, one full of meaning and purpose.

The name of each part or chapter began with a participle, an action-word. May we take action to retrofit our foundations, to find God in all things, to cultivate gratitude, to restore sacrifice, to honor humility and to practice patience. Doing so will lift our spirits, revitalize us and draw us to worship the One who is the "source of all life and holiness."[261]

[261.] "Eucharistic Prayer IV" in the <u>Sacramentary</u>. New York: Catholic Book Publishing Co., 1985, p. 556.

BIBLIOGRAPHY

Amalu, Samuel Crowningburg. Jack Burns: A Portrait in Transition. Honolulu: The Mamalahoa Foundation, 1974.

Beckwith, Martha Warren. Kepelino's Traditions of Hawaii (Bernice P. Bishop Museum Bulletin 95). Honolulu: Bishop Museum Press, 1932.

The Kumulipo: A Hawaiian Creation Chant. Chicago: The University of Chicago Press, 1951.

Berman, Margaret L. Towards a Cultural Architecture: Inquiries into Hawaiian Architecture Prior to 1778. Master of Architecture Thesis, University of Washington, 1994.

Black, Cobey and Mellen, Kathleen Dickenson. Princess Pauahi Bishop and Her Legacy. Honolulu: The Kamehameha Schools Press, 1965.

Bloxam, Andrew. Diary of Andrew Bloxam. Honolulu: Bernice P. Bishop Museum Special Publication 10, 1925.

Brigham, William T. Stone Implements and Stone Work of the Ancient Hawaiians. Honolulu: Bishop Museum Press, 1902.

Cox, J. Halley with Davenport, William H. Hawaiian Sculpture. Honolulu: The University of Hawaii Press, 1974.

Daly, Robert J., S.J. Origins of the Christian Doctrine of Sacrifice. Philadelphia: Fortress Press, 1978.

Fleming, David L., S.J. The Spiritual Exercises of St. Ignatius: A Literal Translation and A Contemporary Reading. St. Louis: The Institute of Jesuit Sources, 1978.

Forbes, David W. Encounters with Paradise. Honolulu: Honolulu Academy of Arts, 1992.

Hawaiian National Bibliography 1780-1900: Vol. I - IV. Honolulu: University of Hawaii Press, 1999-2003.

Fornander, Abraham. Hawaiian Antiquities and Folklore: Vol. VII, No. 1. Honolulu: Bishop Museum Press, 1919.

Fuchs, Lawrence H. Hawaii Pono: A Social History. New York: Harcourt, Brace & World, Inc., 1961.

Gutmanis, June. Na Pule Kahiko: Ancient Hawaiian Prayers. Honolulu: Editions Limited, 1983.

Kahuna La'au Lapa'au: The Practice of Hawaiian Herbal Medicine. Norfolk Island, Austrailia: Island Heritage Limited, 1976.

Handy, E.S. Craighill. Polynesian Religion. Honolulu: Bishop Museum Press, 1927.

Handy, E.S. Craighill and Pukui, Mary Kawena. The Polynesian Family System in Ka-'u, Hawaii. Wellington, N.Z: The Polynesian Society, Inc., 1958.

Handy, E.S. Craighill et al., Ancient Hawaiian Civilization. Rutland, VT: Charles E. Tuttle Co Publishers, 1965.

Harden, M. J. <u>Voices of Wisdom: Hawaiian Elders Speak</u>. Kula, HI: Aka Press, 1999.

Hiroa, Te Rangi (Peter H. Buck). <u>Arts and Crafts of Hawaii</u>: Section XI, Religion. Honolulu: Bernice P. Bishop Museum (Special Publication 45), 1964.

Historical Society, Hawaii. <u>Papers 1-21, 1892-1940</u>. Honolulu: Bernice P. Bishop Museum, nd.

Hitchcock, H.R. <u>An English-Hawaiian Dictionary</u>. San Francisco: The Bancroft Company, 1887.

<u>Ho'okipa: Hawaiian Hospitality</u>. Honolulu: Office of Hawaiian Affairs, 1988.

Hoyt, Helen P. <u>The Night Marchers</u>. Norfolk Island, Australia: Island Heritage Limited, 1976.

'Iokepaokalani, Kahu, S.M. (Fr. Joseph L. Priestly, S.M.), <u>Hawaiian Spirituality</u>. Honolulu: Marianist Hall, 2000.

Irwin, Geoffrey. <u>The Prehistoric Exploration and Colonization of the Pacific</u>. Cambridge: Cambridge University Press, 1992.

Judd, Walter F. <u>Kamehameha</u>. Norfolk Island, Ausralia: Island Heritage Limited, 1976.

Ka'ano'i, Patrick. The Need for Hawaii: A Guide to Hawaiian Cultural and Kahuna Values. Honolulu: Ka'ano'i Productions, 1992

Kamakau, Samuel Manaiakalani. Ka Po'e Kahiko: The People of Old. Honolulu: The Bishop Museum Press, 1987.

Kanahele, George Hu'eu Sanford. Ku Kanaka Stand Tall: A Search for Hawaiian Values. Honolulu: University of Hawaii Press, 1986.

Kelly, Marion. "Some Problems with Early Descriptions of Hawaiian Culture" in Polynesian Culture History, Genevieve A. Highland, Roland W. Force, Allan Howard, Marion Kelly, Yosihiko H. Sinoto, eds. Honlulu: Bishop Museum Press, 1976, pp. 399-410.

Kirch, Patrick V. and Sahlins, Marshall. Anahulu: The Anthropology of History in the Kingdom of Hawaii (Volume Two). Chicago: University of Chicago Press, 1992.

Kittleson, David J. The Hawaiians: An Annotated Bibliography (Hawaii Series No. 7). Honolulu: Social Science Research Institute University of Hawaii, 1985.

Laval, P. Honore. Mangareva: L'Histoire Ancienne D'un Peuple Polynesien. Braine-le-Comte, Belgium: Maison des Peres des Sacres-Coeurs, 1938.

Linnekin, Jocelyn. Sacred Queens and Women of Consequence: Rank, Gender, and Colonialism in the Hawaiian Islands. Ann Arbor: The University of Michigan Press, 1990.

The Liturgy Documents: A Parish Resource, Vol. 1. Chicago: Liturgy Training Publications, 1991.

Long, Max Freedom. The Secret Science Behind Miracles. Los Angeles: Kosman Press, 1948.

Lum, Zita Leimomi Mo'okini, "Religions and Spiritual Movements." A lecture 1982.

"Over the Rainbow." A lecture 26 October 1989.

"We Women and Our Commitments." A lecture at Fort Shafter, January, 1987.

"Children's Day." A presentation preparing for Children's Day 1985.

"Through the Eyes of my Na Kapuna." A lecture at University of Hawaii, 8 April 1975.

Lyman, Richard Ka'ilihiwa. Mea Ho'omana'o: Thoughts. Honolulu: The Estate of Richard Lyman, 1995.

Malo, David. Hawaiian Antiquities (Moolelo Hawaii). Honolulu: Bernice P. Bishop Museum Press, 1951.

Mitchell, Donald D. Kilani, Resource Units in Hawaiian Culture (Fourth Edition). Honolulu: Kamehameha Schools/Bishop Estate, 1992.

Mrantz, Maxine. Women of Old Hawaii. Honolulu: Aloha Graphics and Sales, 1975.

Nakuina, Emma M. and Others. Nanaue the Shark Man and Other Hawaiian Stories. Honolulu: Kalamaku Press, 1994.

Nimmo, H. Arlo, The Pele Literature: An Annotated Bibliography of the English Language Literature on Pele, Volcano Goddess of Hawaii. Honolulu: Bishop Museum Press, 1992.

Palmer, Parker. Let Your Life Speak. San Francisco: Jossey-Bass, 2000.

Peters, Rev. William A.M., S.J. The Spiritual Exercises of St. Ignatius: Exposition and Interpretation. Jersey City: The Program To Adapt The Spiritual Exercises, 1968.

Pukui, Mary Kawena. 'Olelo No'eau: Hawaiian Proverbs and Poetical Sayings. Honolulu: Bishop Museum Press (Special Publication 71), 1983.

Pukui, Mary Kawena and Elbert, Samuel H. Hawaiian Dictionary. Honolulu: University of Hawaii Press, 1986.

Pukui, Mary Kawena, Haertig, E. W. and Lee, Catherine A. Nana I Ke Kumu (Look to the Source), Vol. I and Vol. II. Honolulu: Hui Hanai, Queen Lili'uokalani Children's Center, 1972.

Pukui, Mary Kawena, Handy, E.S. Craighill. The Polynesian Family System in Ka-'u, Hawaii. Rutland, Vermont: Charles E. Tuttle Company, 1972.

Stokes, John F.G. Heiau of the Island of Hawaii: A Historic Survey of Native   Hawaiian Temple Sites. Honolulu: Bishop Museum Press, 1991.

Tachihata, Chieko. Library Resources about Native Hawaiians. Honolulu: University of Hawaii, 1993.

Yardley, Laura Kealoha. The Heart of Huna. Honolulu: Advanced Neuro Dynamics, Inc., 1990.

Yzendoorn, Fr. Reginald, SS.CC. History of the Catholic Mission in Hawaii. Honolulu: Privately Bound Copy, Mo'okini Luakini, Inc., 1926.

Williams, Oscar, ed. Modern Verse: English and American Poetry of The Last 100 Years (from Walt Whitman to Dylan Thomas. Washington Square Press.

CPSIA information can be obtained at www.ICGtesting.com
Printed in the USA
LVOW10s0705240215

428029LV00007B/110/P